•

with the first dream of fire they hunt the cold

•

For Tania,

With best wishes

From

Nov. '[illegible]

Poetry by Trevor Joyce

New Writers' Press
Dublin
Sole Glum Trek
Watches
Pentahedron
The Poems of Sweeny Peregrine
stone floods

Form Books
London
Hellbox

Wild Honey Press
Bray
Syzygy
Without Asylum

with the first dream of fire they hunt the cold

a body of work 66/00

trevor joyce

Published in the Republic of Ireland by
New Writers' Press
61 Clarence Mangan Road
South Circular Road
Dublin 8
Ireland
Website: www.ireland-alive.com/nwp

and in the U.K. by
Shearsman Books
Lark Rise
Fore Street
Kentisbeare
Cullompton
Devon EX15 2AD
Email: shearsman@appleonline.net

Shearsman Books are distributed in the U.S.A. by
Small Press Distribution
1341 Seventh Street
Berkeley
CA. 94710
Email: orders@spdbooks.org
Website: www.spdbooks.org

ISBN 0 907562 29 9

Designed and set by
SoundEye Design
5 Church Street
Cork
Ireland

Printed in Ireland by
ColourBooks Ltd.
105 Baldoyle Industrial Estate
Baldoyle
Dublin

New Writers' Press acknowledges the financial assistance of
An Comhairle Ealaíon / The Irish Arts Council
in the production of this volume

Table of Contents

Acknowledgments

Some of these poems appeared in print in Masthead (Australia), Shearsman (England), Southword (Cork), SVP Magazine (England), Talisman (U.S.A.), The Gig (Canada), The Irish Review, The Irish Times, and The Recorder (U.S.A.), via the 'net in A Chide's Alphabet, and on the web in ND[re]VIEW, The Alsop Review, and The Alterran Poetry Assemblage; I would like to thank the editors responsible.

The range of my indebtedness may be gathered from the dedications associated with many of the poems. In addition to those, however, I want especially to thank Michael Smith and Randolph Healy, my editors at New Writers' Press and Wild Honey Press, respectively, for a personal and poetic commitment way in excess of that function. Alex Davis and George Hitching also gave support when it was needed, and it *was* needed.

My greatest and most particular gratitude, however, is to Angela Conner, whose care saw this into a book, and so it is, finally,

for Angela

The Poems of Sweeny, Peregrine:

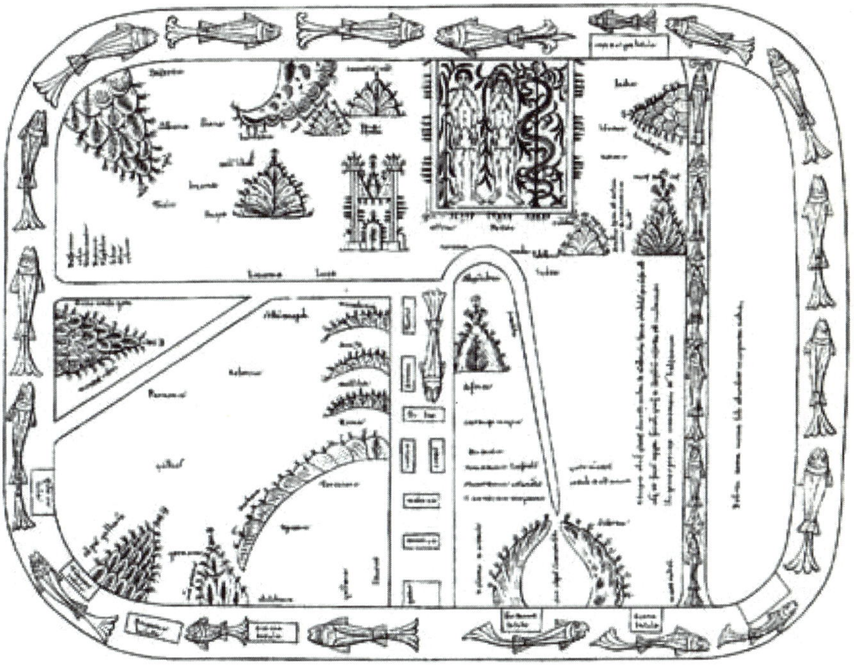

A Working of the Corrupt Irish Text (1966-76)

It's no secret how Sweeny, king of Dal Araidhe and scion of noble though disputed stock, wandered deranged from battle. These periods recount his flight, its reasons and results. These are the records of Sweeny's madness.

There was then in Ireland a cleric called Ronan Finn. A pious and temperate man, he was dedicated to serving his God and opposing the forces of evil.

A time came when he began to plot a church which fell within the area of Dal Araidhe, Sweeny's domain. As the monk circled the boundaries of his site he made such a racket with his handbell that it wasn't long before Sweeny had inquired the source of the strange tolling, and, in a great rage, set out to put an end to Ronan's building. Eorann, his wife, tried to restrain him by grabbing the crimson tassels of his cloak. The fibula sprang from his throat and its precious metal clattered on the floor. His cloak fell limp in the queen's hand as Sweeny made for the church. As yet, only his nakedness was stark.

When Sweeny arrived he found Ronan enumerating the manifold epithets of God from his best psalter. Sweeny snatched that book and tossed it far out into the nearby lake where it tumbled swiftly down the chill waters. Next, as he got set to haul Ronan from the church, he was interrupted by a sudden cry; a servant had arrived from Congal Claon requiring Sweeny to fight at Magh Rath. Left alone as Sweeny and the messenger departed, Ronan bemoaned the loss of his psalter, and recalled with rancour his humiliation.

After a day and a night, a convenient otter fished the psalter up from the bed of the lake and brought it to Ronan. The monk inspected the book and, when he found it intact, began at once to praise God and curse Sweeny, saying: "pray God, naked as Sweeny came let him remain until a spear puts end to such extravagant flight." Then he cursed all Sweeny's kinsfolk; only Eorann was excused, and came in for a blessing.

Ronan next made his way towards Magh Rath, hoping to secure a pact between Domhnall and the tribe of Congal. He did not succeed in this aim; the best he could do was to arrange a truce each night between certain hours. But always the truce was broken; each morning before the hour of battle Sweeny would kill one of Domhnall's men, and he would kill another after the combat ceased at night.

On the day fixed for the deciding battle, Sweeny was first in the field. His skin gleamed through a silken shirt belted with satin. He wore the tunic Congal gave him the day he bested Oilill Cedach; crimson thickly bordered with gold. Chips of carbuncle gemmed its edge and bright silver buttons glinted through loops of silk. Broad heads of iron shod his twin lances, and a shield of tough yellow horn hung at his back. The haft of the sword was worked in gold.

When the other warriors had arrived, and all the great forces were gathered there, Ronan began to go among them with the psalmists of his community. They sprinkled holy water over the assembled ranks and Sweeny received its benefits along with his comrades. Suspicious of being mocked, he slipped his finger through the loop of his iron-tipped spear and with a single blow he killed one of the psalmists. He made another cast then; this time the target of his lance was the monk himself. The blade penetrated the bell on the monk's breast, but the shaft ricochetted, jolting vertically up. Then Ronan spoke: "I invoke the might of God," he said, "that just as that shaft flew high among the upper vapours, you may go also, birdlike, and may your death be by a spear as your spear killed my ward. My curse on you and my blessing on Eorann; and may all the ancient powers bedevil your kin and offspring."

Then the battle was joined. As the vast armies clashed, the warriors grunted and roared, and three times they raised a cry like the loud challenge of a stag, answered and echoed. When Sweeny heard this shrill cacophany rebounding toward him from all sides so that even the sun shook and reverberated in the heavens, he looked up. Troubled then, rage and dread began to grow in him and he became dizzy and a strange restlessness seized him. All the places he knew seemed suddenly repulsive now, and he longed to arrive where he had never been. His fingers trembled and his pulse rushed in his ears as he swayed on weakening legs. His sight was distorted and all his senses dulled when he fulfilled the curse of Ronan. Deranged and rattled as a wild bird, Sweeny began his wanderings.

This commencement of his flight did not disturb even the glittering dew that hung upon the grass; still, crystalline, it lingered. He did not halt on pastureland or rock, in haggard, moor, or dense timber, all of which he passed in that initial flight, but entered the yew-tree of Ros Bearaigh.

Sweeny's kinsmen were routed. It was when their diminished forces passed in their retreat the yew-tree of Ros Bearaigh and tried to cajole him out with promises of wealth that Sweeny, crimson-cloth, whose hair matched the blond adze-flakes, and whose eyes were as blue and flawless ice, rejected them: "you do not know me."

He sprang from the tree into the blind alleys of the rainclouds, remote from roofs and mountains, then travelled Ireland, ferreting chine and gorge, grazing the high jagged cordons of the ivy and tight fissures of stone, from estuary to estuary, among summits and valleys and their recurrence, until he reached the genial Glen Bolcain. Here is the resort of the Irish-turned-maniac, and the glen delights them. Pannage is underfoot, berries abound, and there are many and sweet springs. In simple joy the innocent mad would strike each other down for a choice sprig of cress or a niche to sleep in.

Sweeny dawdled in the glen till one night when he roosted high in an ivy-strangled whitethorn. He couldn't sleep there because each time he twitched the wood tines stuck him, leaving his flesh split and specked with blood. So he went to where a single blackthorn limb spired above a briary thicket, rayed with fine spikes. He perched there, but the slender branch sagged under him and it snapped, throwing him into the thorny mass below so that his skin from heel to head was a crimson tracery. It was thus that Sweeny took a scunner against thorns.

The period of Sweeny's peregrinations between this grievous issuing from Glen Bolcain and his return thereto, was seven years. It was his fastness and his den; women there did not, through thrashing of the yellow flax, recall to him his kinsfolks' thrashing at Magh Rath. Only random care had power to expel him.

Soon in search of him came Loingseachan, a man of close, if uncertain, relation. Beyond any question, though, was his concern for Sweeny, for three times he had retrieved him from out the tortuous courses of his madness. Loingseachan now sought him in the glen, sought him by his prints beside the cress-providing springs, and by the hail of small timber with which his aërial disquietude threatened the timid fauna of the earth. But it was Sweeny who first sighted his pursuer, when he found him asleep in the glen, and he chanted over him the bitter threnodies of his madness.

Shortly the pursuit was resumed with ruse and lure, and Sweeny had occasion in his flight to regret the curse of Ronan Finn. He had recourse to the company of his wife Eorann, whom that cleric had blessed, but he found no haven there. Eorann had taken for husband one Guaire, and the henchmen of this feeble thug drove Sweeny back into the darkness and the frost of which he had made such desperate and formal complaint. The wife of a local erenagh attempted then to beguile him, but shrewdly he eluded her, bidding her tend to her husband and her glebe, and calling to mind their common end. The sharpness of her eyes had troubled him.

He went then to one of the refuges he retained in his homeland, and entered the yew-tree of Ros Earcain. For a month he lived there undetected, but once more there came against him the wily Loingseachan. That man, pigeon and plant, approached the yew, lifting his eyes to the distraught figure on the boughs above. "Sweeny," he began, "I find you here starved, naked on a branch as any bird, with parched lips and a clenched arse. It is hard that this should be the end of one whose body thrilled to silk and dull tunics of satin; once you loosed flickering reins across the necks of foreign stallions, your house held noble youths, fine gentlemen, choice hounds and mastercraftsmen. You dined at many mansions, and countless lords, leaders, squires and hospitallers noted your every whim. Quondam owner of many goblets, with cruets of carved horn for liquors dry and sweet: bird-form now, glimpsed only between wilderness and wilderness. It is hard." At this, Sweeny lingered. He asked for news of his kinsfolk, and Loingseachan, eloquent in his deceit, told him that both his parents were dead, his brother also, and his wife. "A house without a wife," said Sweeny, "is a rudderless boat, is a coat of feathers to the skin, is the kindling of a single fire."

"Dead is your daughter."

"The heart's needle is an only daughter."

"And your only son is dead."

At this last, Sweeny tumbled from the tree and fell to the gyves and shackles of his pursuer.

Locks and fetters were fitted on him and remained, until at last, through manacle and spancel, sense returned. Memory and reason returned to him, as did his figure and appearance; kingship was manifest in him.

When the season of harvest came round, Loingseachan went with his people into the fields. Not so, Sweeny. He was locked deep in an inner chamber of the mill with only the mill-hag for company and warden, and she had been enjoined to silence lest she unsettle the frail sanity of the man. Wilfully, she spoke, inquiring the exploits of his madness. He cursed her, but she led him on, saying the truth should out. She goaded him to leap then; first, over the bed-rail. She matched that. Next through the rooflight of the chamber she followed him, and across the five cantreds of Dal Araidhe, until wearily he roosted on an ivy-branch in Fiodh Gaibhle, the hag beside him.

It was the end of the harvest-time precisely. The cry of the hunt and the bellow of the running stag carried through the wood; Sweeny suppressed his initial fright and chanted of the trees of Ireland, and of his grief.

This done, he took off once more across the summits of the land, and each leap was mimicked by the hag until at last he sprang from the battlements of Dun Sobairce and she faltered in pursuit; she fell upon the sea-cliffs and the rock broke her. A catspaw played with her wreck.

Fearful then of Loingseachan's vengeance, he wandered on, coming at last to the land of the Britons. He held the castle of the king of that land upon his right side and came upon a forest, wherein he heard sounds of lamentation and anguish. Sweeny entered the forest and found there another madman, the Man of the Wood. Each recited the aetiology of his derangment, and the two entered upon a contract of friendship: "Sweeny," said the other, "we have exchanged confidences, now each must be the other's guard; he who attends the crane's call break above the blue and turquoise waters, who hears the lucid cry of cormorants, the clatter of a woodcock's wings, snapping of spent wood, or sees birds' shadows on the roofing boughs, let him give warning; two tree-trunks shall divide us and if either hears any of these things or similar, then let us flee, swiftly."

For a year they were together; then the Man of the Wood had, perforce, to go to where his death awaited him, to be snatched by a gust into a waterfall to drown. He delayed only until Sweeny had told him his own tale just as it is set down hereinafter, then sought out that fatal and elementary conjunction, and the fall included him.

Sweeny went back to Glen Bolcain. There a madwoman pursued him until Sweeny divined her madness and turned, whereupon she fled before him. This he made the subject of his chant, strophe and shrill counterstrophe.

He did not stand. His course brought him back to the home of his old wife Eorann, where again he came to grief; she, seeing his wretchedness, rejected him. On Benn Boirche, a peak among the southern ranges, he found such rest as he could take, victim of storm and graupel, and retold the shifting numbers of his ways.

At firstlight he entered again upon his route; he crossed the green and limpid Shannon, saw the sublime Sliabh Aughty as he made his way to Bile Tiobradain in east Connaught. That night the snow came down, and as it fell it froze, drift upon drift. "Though it be the death of me," said Sweeny, "better to suffer philanthropy than such incessant pain." In this form, a gleam of reason came then to the nearly reclaimed haggard; but it was revealed to Ronan Finn that Sweeny had come to, and would return amongst his people. Adamant through time, the monk renovated his curse: "let him have no relief from your just vengeance, Lord, till death," and the Lord obliged.

At midnight Sweeny halted at the centre of Sliabh Fuaid, and there beheld an apparition. Bloody truncated torsos, their lopped heads leaping beside them, gibbered and brawled on the path, and five of them, heads grizzled and hirsute, lacked torso or trunk between them. He heard their chat:

"He's mad," said the first head.

"A madman of Ulster," said the second.

"Let us hunt him," said the third.

"Long let the hunt be," said the fourth.

"To the sea," said the fifth, and they lifted towards him; headlong he fled.

The call of that hunt was the din and stridulation of stark terror and the hubbub of the chivvying spectres. They butted and plucked at his calves, ankles, shanks, shoulders and nape, clashing with branches, rocks, and each other like a flood unleashed and falling. At last he hid in the high gauze of the clouds, to be sure to be sure that he had lost them; both human heads and those of dog and goat which had been intermingled.

Such was the most strenuous of Sweeny's flights, and for three fortnights after he didn't halt from his career long enough even to drink.

Another of Sweeny's demented journeys took him from Luachair Deaghaidh to where the serene waters of Fiodh Gaibhle doubled its bright blossom. For a year he fed upon the blood-red and the saffron berries of the holly-trees, the dark earth-colours of the acorns, and clear water, then his grief returned upon him and he took up his chant.

He was diverted only briefly then by the cliff of Farannan, but was pleased enough by its ivy and apple-trees, and by the wild deer and the ponderous swine of the valley, and the fat seals snoring on the wrack below, and so he praised it.

Soon he came to where Moling was reading to his students; he lay at the edge of the spring and began to crop the water-cress. The saint greeted him, saying that his arrival was foreknown, as, also, his death in that place. Further, he bound the madman that, however far he might travel by day, each night he would return so that his tale might be set down.

This, for a year, was his routine, and each night he attended vespers with the saint. Moling instructed Muirghil, wife of his swineherd Mongan, to give Sweeny some of each day's milking. It was her habit to thrust her heel into the pat of cowdung nearest her, and fill the depression with new milk; surreptitiously, Sweeny would steal into the vacant yard to lap up the proffered meal.

Muirghil fell out one evening with another woman. Out of sheer spite the other accosted Mongan next day as Muirghil was pouring the milk into the dung and Sweeny watched from the hedge beside. "Coward," she said, "there's a man at your wife in the bush over there." The jibe aroused his anger, and he snatched up a spear from the rack and made for the hedge.

Sweeny's flank was towards him as he lay feeding from the dung. The herd lunged, the blade penetrated the rib-cage beside the right nipple and so shattered the spine. Or was it perhaps the tine of a deer's antler which the herd had concealed at Sweeny's trough which did the irreparable harm?

Whichever the case, when the deed was reported to Moling he came with retinue of clerics to the place where Sweeny lay, and there administered all appropriate sacraments.

It was then that the stricken man uttered his final chant as the death-swoon softened him and he could no longer sustain the rigorous discipline of his derangement. He lasted long enough only to be enjambed across the threshold of the church, whereupon death took him. He was interred by Moling with the inevitable rites.

Moling it was who first recorded this tale of Sweeny, and noted his chants, but it is uncertain to how great an extent that saint expressed his reverence for the silent dead by emendation of a strange and confused history, and how far editors and critics have conspired with him, and time, and chance, to make corruption of the word outpace that of the flesh. Perhaps a final turn was added too, to make a palinode. May we, then, conclude just this: that, after all, we have not here those words which Sweeny, between flight and fall, spoke to the Man of the Wood?

I

God has given me life;

without music, without rest,
without woman's company,
loveless
he gave me life,

and so you find me here
living disgraced in Ros Bearaigh;
the life God gave
seems somehow dislocated.

You do not wish to know me.

II

The blackthorn drinks my blood again,
my face bleeds on the sodden wood.

Flood and ebb encompass me;
lunar phases can't affect
the homicidal iron I dread.

Thorns lance my sores. I doze.

III

Is it the cold that wakes me;
can deadly iron draw near through dream?

Here night is palpable. – Listen!
hear the sound of mounted men
thunderous through the echoing wood;
have they my imminent death in mind?

Only the rain throbs on the grass.

IV

My lids still slack,
a year of fearful nights has made them
heavy as lids of gold.

Christ, king of saints, hear me,
this is no fate for a monarch.
What dignity is there in this,
dodging between tree and tree?

My feet are open sores.
Two black suns
burn in my face
and my raw lips pulse
like edges of a wound.

V

This clearing is too open,
without trees;
I am vulnerable here
without spear or shield.

I have no weapons;
I know no women in Glen Bolcain.

Listen to the wind.
No deft fingers jerk the lutestring.

The blackthorn bears new fruit tonight:
an insane king.

His blood becomes its sap,
flowing like water.

VI

I am too weak for wars,
mine is a complete poverty;
snow sits next neighbour to the bone
of pauper and energumen.

There is no further hindrance in the night
which snow-blind eyes anticipate;
ice and wood
have thrown up palisades against me,
blossoms can lacerate the flesh.
Pathways of this dementia
writhe, serpentine, on earth.

My pale paunch juts
from a torn and threadbare vest:
I am Sweeny of Ros Earcain,
call me Sweeny crazed.

The ice-sharp wind lances me through,
the snow has left me red and raw;
upon this gale I drift to death
that dangles from each twisted tree:
fear has enervated me,
left me frenzied in Glen Bolcain.

VII

Madness shrieks beneath my feet
as I search for watercress.

Madness lurks among the reeds
leaping at me when I stoop
about a hill-pool.

Madness has a white and haggard face.

VIII

When the livid sky is swollen with thunder
and the reeds ache beneath the pelting hail;
then you may see the proud, the noble Sweeny
dragging his sodden rags across blue flesh.

IX

In summertime the blue-grey herons stand
rigid above sharp waters.

In wintertime the wolfpacks
thread the snow-glens with their spoor,
and with their moaning they thread the long wind.

I hear their snow-blurred howling
as I cross the iron lakes
and crack the frost from my beard.

X

Frost stands in the air
ice grips the bone;
ice holds half the doubled moon:
snow is coldest
before dawn.

Nothing delays, my love,
decay of crimson cloth.
On bleak plateaux
snow and the wind
undressed me long ago;
cruel sempstress briar
confounds seam and suture,
sews my skin with wood.

Sweeny possessed
is Sweeny dispossessed
of glib and dazzling wife.
Do not, therefore,
distress yourself
who once were
subject of my
sad distraction;
with you, good love,
I harvest tares.

You and the thorn
still mortify
proud flesh.
For a down bed
I am abandoned
and unanswerèd;

the falcon does not brood
upon such mutes.
Chanting, I will stoop and bind
upon a field of air.

Brambles cast
sly nets of wood;
the air is thorned with frost:
before dawn always
wind is sharpest.

XI

You whose thorned orbs fix me
know I am a fallen image;

dulled and scarred since war
is Sweeny, the pre-eminent:

stay house-held and husbanded;
our paths, co-terminal. Woman, I go.

XII

Life is loud in the glen.

Frail stag,
            your cry has halted me;
now I am sick with sudden longing:

odour of herds from pasturelands,
stag bold in crag and sky.

Oak, broad and leafy spire;
good fruit bends the hazel wands.

Gap stopped with dappled boughs,
bright alder boughs;
there are no blood specks on my skin
as I move on.

Blackthorn: barbed wine. And this
above the pool and on the pool, sparse
and sour green,
                        cress.

Saxifrage and oyster-grass
are a green path. and see
this ochre, fallen fruit,
this apple-tree.

Mountain blossom. Mountain ash.
My flesh has dropped in a crimson net;
briar, drunk-thorn briar.

Yew is the little churchyard tree,
and where the night of wood congeals
the ensnarled darkness is named 'ivy'.

In hollyboughs I hide from storms,
I hide from the clubbed ash too.

Verge of a dark wood,
vertical chalked motif,
slender, silver, coiling, lovely
birch.

Aspen is swift; its leaves
sing like a distant war;
green blade smashes green blade.
Then, for a time,
                    silence.

In forest glades
my dread:
oakwood pendulous in wind.

XIII

Mountains are rivered slopes,
brown rock and scree;
I would sleep if I were let
in green twilight of Glen Bolcain.

Water; light through green glass,
wind bright as glancing steel,
the ouzel sips the vivid spring,
cress green as the ocean's ice.

Slopes littered with tough ivy,
thin willows blade the mirrored streams,
yews are intense and many there,
birch is the dim glen's lamp.

No act could hold me, Loingseachan;
I would break frosted routes up Boirche.

You were a scabbard of iron words:
father and mother
daughter and son
and brother dead;

supple sweet body,
bright wife
gone to earth.

I am a cave of pain.

XIV

Dense wood is my security,
the ivy has no edge.

Though the lark pursues me,
summed, I take the dove
that crosses, and am no red hawk.
Shadow of the rising woodcock,
blackbird's scream, disturb me.

I stoop to see the little fox
a-worrying of the butchered bones;
he has more shifts to seize me than the wolf.
The guileful fox, the murderous wolf I shun,
scumber and filth befoul them.

Light folds and bends in the chill ice
of pools, and I am cold.
Still, the heron is at sedge,
the badgers squeal in Benna Broc.

Here there are ample stags
to turn much fallow with the share,
but no hand holds
the stag of high Sliabh Eibhlinne,
the stag of sharp Sliabh Fuaid,
the stags of Ealla and of Orrery,
the fierce stag of Loch Lein,
the stag of twin-spurred Baireann;
each stands at rest on salient ground.

Sweeny, I, swift visitant of glens;
rather, call me Man Run Through.
O stag, I could lie down
among your jagged tines
in pointed luxury;
now I await the final point.

See the royal stag go by
dressed in his tattered velvet.

Ronan Finn compelled me here.

XV

My sleep is sad
without feather-bed, numb
from the sharp air
and the grit of the wind-blown snow.

Cold wind with ice,
ghost of an old sun,
shelter of a single tree
on this barren table-land.

Striding through rainstorms,
pacing the mountain deer-paths
and paths through grass
in the orange frost at dawn;
stags are belling
in forest copses,
the paths of the deer are sheer and hard:

I hear the hammer of the distant surf.

O great God above
my weakness is also great
and black are the sorrows of Sweeny
whose scrotum hangs slack.

XVI

Four winds fetch many miles
to meet in me, am as a fifth,
fluent and cold. Boirche
is perilous: so deep
its silent reaches, power
of secret currents threatens me.

I have not yet forgotten
harvest-time in Ulster
around quivering Lough Cuan;

I have lived in Ossory
and within the glades of Meath,
now their springs inhabit me;
in the aftermath of fruit
observe such exaltation:

I sift the debris of the shattered woods.

XVII

I occupy in alien woods
an old retreat;
in my familiar square of trees
shrewd centre of such intimate quincunx am I
whistle of a woken plover
is unsettling plangency.

Secure amid a lasting drift of leaves
I graze on mast and sorrel.
Hazards are these:
shy doves agog in upper branches,
cormorant's disturbance.

Where heron calls cold waters move,
my soft co-occupant of woods.

XVIII

Enmity is sorrow.

Better be stillborn,
better a misbirth, slight sprawling foetus,
than bear enmity.

There is seldom a league of three
but one murmurs;
blackthorn and briar have wounded me
so it is I who murmur.

The crazed woman fears her man;
mine is a curious story,
as the naked man, his feet unshod,
hides from the fearful woman.

When the wild duck and the autumn
move among the glades and lakes,
and the woodlands glow like thickening honey;
then it is good to rest, cradled in the gloom of ivy.

Whosoever bears enmity,
whether man or wife,
whosoever bears enmity,
may he die eternally.

Glen Bolcain has bright waters;
I have heard it loud with birds
and foaming streams
and the lisp of river-surf on reefs.

Holly and the close wands of its hazel
have sheltered me; berries and nuts
acorns and blue velvet sloes,
these have fed me.

Its woods are quick with hounds,
and the stag, at gaze, barks;
all is mirrored in the lucid waters.

I did not hate it.

XIX

My madness finds congruity
on the frozen peak of Boirche;
but what milk or bread sustains
flesh invaded by the snow?

A strait bed sprung with frost
straddles the barren rock,
branches play bone
to wasted limbs.

In a cage of ice
I pace the bars
while frost-buds mimic sweat.

I give fire to the glinting wind.

As the snow succeeds the hail
in autumn I, precipitate,
abandon chasms
of oblique basalt
for zones less igneous,
less cold: replete
anfractuous Glen Bolcain.

Four gaps to the wind
define the glen;
its fertile woods,
its frigid springs
trapped in sheer pits.

Through clear pools gravel spins
in a shifting vortex,
cress and brooklime
dip their leaves
to make a green meniscus.
Beyond, as in, Glen Bolcain
drenched earth tonight is frozen,
but no marauder breaks
the glen's secure horizon.

Bitter leaves
drift among berries there,
garlic and the wild onion
exhale their pungent steam
against the iridescence of the sloes,
and underfoot the path
is frail with acorns.

See, in decaying groves, a king
who stumbles among pawns.

XX

I am miserable
Sweeny,
bone and blood
are dead;
sleepless;
storm-sound
is the only music.

Luachair Deaghaidh
to Fiodh Gaibhle
journeying,
fed on the ivy-crop
and oakmast;
a twelvemonth on this mountain,
aviform,
gorged on the saffron holly-fruit.

Berserk
in Glen Bolcain,
my anguish is
patent,
my strength is worn away tonight,
I have cause for grief.

XXI

Cliff of Farannan,
abode of saints; with many hazel groves
and nuts in cluster; quick icy brooks
that sprinkle down its walls: there are green cords
of ivy, a rich mast of acorns
and the apple-trees,
heavy with good fruit they arc
their boughs.
Many badgers make their setts and the lithe hare
shelters there, the seals gather in
from the open sea.

I am Sweeny,
son of Colman the Just.
I have lain weak
beneath many frostfalls;
Ronan of Druim Gess outraged me.

I shall rest beneath some tree
at that far
waterfall.

XXII

I once thought that the quiet speech
of people held less melody
than the low throating of doves
that flutter above a pool.

I thought the bell
by my elbow not so sweet
as the fluting of the blackbird to the mountain
or the bellow of a hart in the storm.

I thought the voice
of a lovely woman less melodious
than the dawn-cry
of the mountain grouse.

I thought the yowling
of the wolves more beautiful
than the baa and bleat
of a preaching priest.

Though in your chapel you find melody
in the quiet speech of students,
I prefer the awesome chant
of Glen Bolcain's hounds.

Though you relish salted hams
and the fresh meat of ale-houses,
I would rather taste a spray of cress
in some zone exempt from grief.

I am transfixed; the iron
intrudes on shattered bone.
Tell me, God who sanctions all,
why did I survive Magh Rath?

Though each bed I made
without duplicity was good
I would rather inhabit familiar stone
above Glen Bolcain's wood.

I give thanks to you, Christ,
for partaking of your body;
in my death I truly repent
all my evil deeds.

Pentahedron
&
others
(1966-76)

in memoriam
Louis Aldonse Donatien
de Sade

The existence of a rose is a violence.
Francis Bacon

The Moon as Other than a Green Cheese

Tonight
a phosphorescence is toddling along the night
having the form
of a silver apple, walking pome.
at sight
of paling slopes its light
dims and drowns among the crystallizing domes
that swell into the dawn among the drone
of wasps and errant ichneumons, only
a few caterpillars have wandered
tranced by a phosphorescent pome.

River Tolka and Botanical Gardens

Eggshells of white hoar crackled underfoot.

Shrill alarm-cries speared the wind
as a blackbird jotted across the snow.
black asterisks marked its progress.

A heavy-timbered pine groaned,
swung, slowly straightened; while,
as echo, other trunks heaved in the wind
like huge, half-buried torsos.

Below, a carcass in the snow,
smirched snow, rat's blood upon it,
crushed rat's bone upon it,
splintered on the bone-pale snow,
rat's marrow.

The snow turned grey. lights slanted
in cold hollows, dark waters flowed on.
and dark, below swart boughs, a rat lay,
much too cold to rot.

The Importance of the Bells
(Meath St. Church)

The bells are born and die
becoming part of history
along with
the French Revolution,
two world wars,
Lawrence of Arabia,
and the death of the cat
who is posing dramatically
in the gutter.

Acts are expectorated,
and when the spittle hardens
into facts, our lives
are emerald threads of mucus.

The clamorous life of the bells
is short and eventful,
comprehensive of squalor
and of the drab other
ways of living.

The disembodied tones
finger carp on a slab
and the red necks
awry in a poulterer's window;
frenetic search for pattern
before giving up the ghost.

The angelus has rung,
surely somewhere a seed quickens.

The results of this act follow.
fish-wife wipes her hands
on a fish-grey apron,
crosses herself. an urchin
crossing the street
to inspect a corpse in the gutter
stops
to register the eighteen chimes.

And the steel-blue, gutted fish
insistent on the facts of life.

Dead Man's House

This morning he shrugged his skin off,
a scarecrow, robbed of cross-struts,
flesh fell down. grey eyes, grey face,

white with a thousand maggots, will make
black clay. the still air insinuates death
between the flute of blackbirds on the roof.

and dogs and children calling in the street;
an agony of innuendoes, of significant pauses.

the television aerial is a question mark
and the blackbirds are periods, it reads
like a telegram whose meaning eludes us.

I find some details in my mind
stamped 'dead' and dated for today.

part of my brain is dead
and will rot within a twelvemonth.

An Execution Remembered

A decapitated chicken bolted
across the yard, scattering gouts
from its blunt neck. the blood seeped
between my closed lids and even
into the sun which returned it

in a fine spray, making rubies
of dull stones. the bird convulsed,
sternum jerked on the earth, back and forth,
punctual as a pendulum; metronome
for the rhythmic pace of the butcheress

with the bright axe. since then she died,
dignified as a headless pullet.
the sun makes scarlet stained-glass
of my eyelids, still throbbing
like an ubiquitous metronome.

Construction

A. 1. I had just turned off from Stephen St.
Into Great Ship St., was confronted
By a massive grey stone wall.

The late rain lay in patches
On the pavements, shone
Between the grey-green cobbles

Of the roadway, throwing up
Grey facets of built stone.

2. The cobbles were enamel,
Chipped away in places,
Showing the basic texture
Underneath; grey rock.

B. 1. This was suave ceramic
Fired in the mind's furnace.
I had to look again.

2. Each individual limestone cuboid
Chisel-squared and weathered
Rough and grimy, holding on its face
All its past history and the threat
Of its future. Streams
Of rust-brown rain had stained
The entire wall; each
Block realized its presence

In this pattern and the wider
Patterns of sunlight, shadows, tone
And the complete distributed
Weight of rock
Combined for the present.

C. My brain had built
A scheme of echoes,
Of ancient meanings held
In rock, in sunlight on ice,
In the low beginnings of thunder

But this wall needed no exterior
Aid for its stability,
No echo in its circumstance.

Gulls on the River Liffey

The river, between bridges, lies rectangular,
A sheet of filthy linen, green on grey cement.

The concrete is arranged in geometric planes
And the river's sides and angles make similar shapes.

All is superstructure here, no gaps between forms
Through which to glimpse the basic groundplan of the scheme.

The gulls are not rectangular. Their cries contrast
With the street's stochastic drone.

The gulls drift in sequence; existence certified
By the first bridge, their absence by the second.

The river moves and does not move,
And the gulls have a similar movement and a stasis.

Surd Blab

I Vespers flood the evening roads,
troubling the violet halflight
between walls and hoardings

where plaster, paint and torn advertisements
creep from their places and beneath
new surfaces are moistened in their turn.

Here between memorials and neon signs
I look to find the question
which the stone and glass would answer
falling inward from their places into one.

If only that question would emerge –
but it hides
like a child at play, half-hidden
by a lamp-post, peering
round to see who follows,

running ahead,
shrieking shrill laughter.

II

Between the stark oak-boles up on the hill
a grey smoke of drizzle hangs, grey
as the hard rind of wood-lice, grey
as the dull top of a lake in storm.

The bright beads slipping down the wood,
each an imploded cosmos, but bright
and the chatter of the nettles under mist
could be a dream of shrieking children.

III Cold and opaque
as a chunk of river quartz,
the town that inroads these eyes.

The effort to impress
rock results
in the quick fixed,

or a fossil mote
sprouting in our late
damp climate.

The hazel leaves,
the hazel wands
scream in storm winds.

Words are blown
in the storm like old saurian
down.

An innocent, profane
joy floods through and down
painfully.

There is a problem in the still
adjacent stone
and the river's blab.

IV This hour is delicate,
a pink-gold shell with an ocean in it,
a whorl,
a frozen whirlpool.

This is my hour,
see, I have charted it,
it is mine.

A million deeds
centre here
and a million
of my futures.

It is expressly mine
this whorling hour,
this iridescent spiral.

But who can bend a spiral
to a question mark?

That question is the present deed.

V It is the question
of framing the problem
that disturbs me
now that laughter's muted.

It is the surd
that links opposing
corners of the world-box
that troubles now,

That has snowballed.
It is a question of a
question of a question
etc. The mouths are silent now,

mute in hiding.

Diagram + Sun

A thin gravel of coal,
of grain and shattered glass
glistening preciously
in the shadow of a slag-heap,
in the huge darkness of a crane.

that circles the sun
like a searching blade.

Grouping doves
stab after corn here
and the shape of the high gnomon
plays across their plumaged
dove-grey heads and subtle breasts
and gradually the chipped glass
dulls; the prisms sift no more
bright fluids and the waters
slow.

Through hours the river halts,
reverses and the dredgers swivel round,
dragging their stern-ropes out.
the rustle of a tautening hawser
furrows the sapphire dusk.

A lissom fog vaulted the debrised channel
to see its shape scored glaucously.
the tart air moults a sultry ash.

Tight bars of steel
mount like elongated boulders.
a golden bird swoops
to its eyrie
high on the cragged metal.

A sabre crane-boom scabs
the throbbing blue aorta
in a brutal pivot.

Two locked sparrows drop
out of an alley's mouth;
the small grenade squawked,
fractioning,
jolting the feathers down
onto the river's skin
to be sloughed
in another ocean
and another time.

And someone,
                    maybe a child,
                              asked;
'aren't birds strange'
                    and
'has the sun bled all away?'

Schedule of Monuments

The Greeks held that the soul hid in the belly
        near the heart.
the ones I know are locked in bone.

I met a madman in the park,
        beneath the silver fountain,
        who recounted old obscenities
        on halted breath.
He had a world inside his skull
        and even fogs of alcohol could not obscure
        malevolence of water, stone and light
        and other eyes whose gaze defined
        the deranged orbit of his pain.
His voices thickened in his throat
        and through the orifice in his skull
        echoed his anguish. maybe so

he mirrors us
and when the world booms in your brain
        where do you run for resonant fear?
around and round a cage of bone
        in great cycles of history.
        cycles of birth and growth
        and birth and growth: and death?

Jesting Pilate did not wait
        to hear the hollow bone reverberate
        with echoes of his curious wit.

but we will wait and wait and wait
        to hear our words come back;
        crouched, propped on thighbones,
        skeletal pyramids, late kingdom.

Chronicle

Boots shapeless with ochre mud and heavy; our gear a neutral grey, stiff with impregnated dirt: our history in metals blood and dust.

The rhythm of our steps faltered on the silent air. Footfall and echo, layer on layer they spread behind us a wake of loudening thunder.

Eyes in their black orbits, low waters of a bitter well; and mouths clogged with long dumbness hold no explanation. Exterior thunder drowns all whispers down; useless to question.

Shock of dull impact, on the ground a crimson necklace glitters, red globules form in ruts and harden; beads of red glass. Speech is a broken bird on stunned wings. The smashed hawk lies now, neck askew on the caked earth:

and explanations are irrelevant. We have observed our outer skins moult in white fluttering shreds and felt the sting of wind with weary eyes: but yet we move.

Compulsively. Our limbs and senses grope tentacular; things are involved, indrawn; made monuments in a circular landscape. And some of us made songs

about the journey in our minds.

Death is Conventional
(song, probably evasive)

For us, to know is to participate. Perceiving is building. The peceiving of life – indissolubly – is the construction of life – the rebuilding *of it.*
S. Eisenstein

The eye lifts, strong as a hawk in the open sun
the flame comes,
                                        flame of the song;
clay falls from the mouth
and the looping skin breaks,
prison of bone is gone in the hot flood
and no habit shields the heart,
                                                            the life
that has come to terms.

but fact is coy,
tongue is a fox,
                              flagrant and slim.

Fire needs no convention for existence,
fire needs no habit and no gesture,
though fear may hunt like a spider, quick,
fire is intense and huge.

germ in the air; short egg of sound,
flame of the life. the eye and voice.

While we speak
                                    leaves turn and fall;
earlier even than the dawn,
                                                      orange through frost,
the click of thawed ice from my window-glass,
                                                      (the passage turns)
each pane grew bright from the centre out
and the day dilated like a lung.

the sun returns,
                              falling like snow.

A neighbour died in the first cold spell;
(gutted wreckage after fire)
quick rodent eyes; restless
                                                  with smaller life.

how come to terms?
                                      what compromise?
(death is most vivid)

No flame in the fields.
ragwort,
                grey ash:
cut briar has no growth.
cattle break ice to drink,
                                              low sun.
small fire;
                    a cask of fungoid apples in the barn.
rooks in the near elms
                                          are louder,
more ponderous of wing
                                            (shot,
dangling from a pole,
                                            they made an excellent scarecrow
on an orange wall of corn)
fox runs by now,
                              nearer to the door.
flame-like evasive celebrant.

Narcissus,
                    leaning above the pool
alone,
              loving himself;
thought froze into a pallid bloom.

eyeless,
                    not noticing the change,
Narcissus
                    wondered at the sudden night.

brain made thin stamens,
spathe was of bone; life
compressed to vegetable fibre
complex of memory and future.

Narcissus pseudo-Narcissus.

gone subtly,
                    like the fox to earth,
the dead neighbour made no matter
to this synthetic, pensive flower.

a storm-wrecked elm caved the roof,
and the rooks held open house.
the children moved away. (the elm rotted)
others forgot and died.

Narcissus changed into a flower,
the bubble of the skull burst.
all the iridescing lights
and glancing plays of sun
reverted into water, fire and earth.

they traced their patterns on the leaves,
no longer understood or felt
until the sap froze in the stem
bursting the turgid cells.

Cul-de-sac words. parables: fraud.

how come to terms?
                                        how compromise?

the rooks are garrulous and strong
the fox is strong as fire.
                                        how celebrate?

abroad upon the early snow
a blackbird stammers at the sun
as it goes slowly up the east
and makes the rooftops glare bright gold.

break from ancestral dead, sweet incense flesh:
break mouth in wordless song.
grand fierce daughter of those dead, strong bolt of fire,
repository of gentle song. drunk in midwinter, brazen
with winter sun. subtly to mutual earth come;
child of the grey, slipping moon; in fire.
furnaced life. urned death. no words.

so we participate in death.

Christchurch. Helix. 9th Month.

Passages of labyrinth repeat;
the crypt gives vellum thighs to the dead,
mark our return in this way;
again we hollow dust-caves, ankle-deep.

Paths are furrowed by rats' feet,
scribbled as cryptic schemes, motifs
of death and propagation;
here the fruit of death dilates.

Arid courses interplay, rivers of dust,
graphs wrought in frost, dust-falls interpret sunlight.
A cat plays knucklebones with something grey
and we move into daylight:

for mornings the roads are chrome
and the sun is a citron stain on a limed wall.

The Fall

I have mouthed names
        that are names no longer,
draw no reply now
        only hard silence and an image
                of graven stone.

Yew-trees, evergreen,
        viridian intensity of growth;
                gravity derived from dirt.

The names draw no reply,
        only a silence in the mind,
                movement of smoke.
familiar shadows that are only smoke.

The sun marks time
        among the evergreens:
                posture of green fire.

Stone cracked in the jaws of ice,
        splintered, grinding,
                mixed with moisture,
becoming dirt.

There is no grave memorial in carven stone.
        There is one gravity.

The names falling from use
        down into stone,
        down into my mind.
There is no grave memorial in the future of my mind.

All names will fall from use.

Twin Relative Deposition

2 years of watches remark the end of autumn

Subtle as the leaking stench of gas
that trembles the slight web of sleep
they died; and so quick the dead
lose their composure, moulting age with face.
all habit broken and all gesture discontinued.

The dandelion, frost-quenched, watches in the house,
marks time along the well-path; lion's-tooth
that emptied cheek and jaw of meat,
hiding in the hollow house now, waiting
near the well where the neighbours don't go now.

Soon even the memory will be gone,
the old woman and her brother will be a broken habit;
the neighbours will compose new plots;
the well-path will be overgrown;
well forgotten, covered by a policy of growth.

Lion's-tooth, famished at the acrid lakeside,
re-mounts to the village as the mercury drops:

oil bright in a crock,
        flame tilting at the wick;
                blue-herons in a bladed bay.

                last autumn month.

Dynamic

Above the fog a gibbous moon is growing
    or, farther on, a nebula bursts.

Beneath, before an urgent train,
    deliberately a body breaks;
    frail as an arrow from an iron bow.

and countless wheels revolve
    on distant rails towards vacant junctions
    whose cries
    issue and are lost in the blind watches of the night.

Air shifts; the fog bends from the brightening stream
    where scales glint between reaches thick with sedge.

but in the towns the streetlamps, brutal and bright as lions,
    prowl through the lifting mists
    and each eye traps in brilliant lids
    a carnage or a void.

All forms are savaged as they come:
    maimed men who limp on club-leg,
    garroted men with meths-blue faces,
    women whose secretive survival
        shuns the predatory light,
    and all the ashen faces of the dead.

Forms hatched in anonymous darkness, sane,
    spawn into light;
    quick life from thickening fungus,
    spores of pain.

Beyond the fog the harvest moon
    lifts its fullness through an empty sky.

                    the rails are cleared of incongruity and blood.

                         the seasonal change approaches.

The Roads, People, the River (Soured with Industrial Excrement) & Town:

What more reason for a bird's rapture
than in the silent passage of quiet people
whose dark labyrinth only comprehends them:

first night of spring; the wind
is white and full, the moon
is only a direction, without edges
or exact location in this long fall;

a radio speaks in a window's mouth
and it is not for such verbed symbols
working across the road's dumb ceaseless fall
their weave, their patterned maze,

that the beggar's hands are veined with lead,
his body without redolence of lilies,
nor that some windows lack familiar light now,
and flowers must be found, even in such snow;

by the distillery wall the vagrant's breath
grips on the frozen stone, the moon
is the white bird on his shoulder;
as sound, presence and colour, dragging

like golden ants upon their backs their own apprehension,
flock into his skull and make their nest, and breed,
what more reason for a bird's rapture?

Parallax

Figures group on the frozen square,
into the black shadow of the flats;

dark path of snow from the abattoir:
sills of an old debtors' prison
double this red-gold dusk.

call of a woman, a withered star,
falls, broken, through the resonant light.

Time Piece. Clocks Err through Anger of the Watcher

Bell-towers beat the hours of night,
gathering the measured growth
in sheaves of violent dark blooms.

in the third hour, below St. Patrick's,
a woman, about sixty,
started a drunken dance for the moon
and her laughter lit the angry houses
and by-passers, going toward town,
crossed over from incongruous joy
as frost tightened on the city.

fourth hour, the river turns.
bells leap along the walls
like vagrant gulls,
shocking the lovers out of arms
reach. they return
out of the metal night
into their hour of silent laughter.

when the moon set
and the stars wheeled through precise darkness
a child was laughing
up into the sky
soaring and japing like a playful rook
into the blind socket of the moon.
tumult of black scarlet roses
between stars and warehouse walls.
a windowed flame: a vigil, premonition disobeyed.
ice burns like fire; eyes sad and the dawn comes.
river, a scythe beneath the bridge
reaping a startled flock of gulls.
fire in the mouths of vigil-keepers,
fire in the mounting sun.

your strong words break echoes from
the walls and vacant squares.
anguish of life bound in your flesh.
anger of roses full of storm,
anger in pitching bells
and in the hammer of the sea,
anger of blood: your look suffused with darkness,
anger of love
fluid among casing frosts.
and the lanes and walls,
the cathedral and canal
burn with the force of echoes.

the clocks segment another hour.

silver foliage is winter fire
under a red vague sun.
turrets of ice, reeds chime
like a nest of wasps. another hour.

the sun floats hooded on the frozen air.

Pentahedron

I In the soft dark rain
the presence of the sleeping man
is sensed only by dogs.
they scent and whine.

Stars have grown up in the sky like fruit,
the moon corrodes, the moon
falls like ash and smoulders;
sourness of acid rain.

When your lips are falling through the ruined jaw
they will remember autumn
and the painful fruit.

Go now into the central squares
(prison of statues, great as trees,
whose gestures spread above our heads
like branches through contorted air).

When your lips melt from the bone
and rats sip from your skull's trough
then they will fear the vagrant's dream,
recall his song.

The impregnable marble bodies;
in the rain the blind eyes weep.
again through close oppressive night
the soft beak nags the shell.

II The way from school is across the bridge
where pregnant waters kiss green stone
and on the plinth where an old man sleeps
slogans of love dissolve.

Look where the sun has entered the canal
and summer decorates the railway track
quake-grass above the gentle moss
responds to tepid rain.

Torture of the word and understanding
pain of the flesh in song:
the mouth, unanswered, falls away,
sorrow,
          and the beat of rain.

Yet the sleeper does not wake.
in the narrow lanes by the cathedral
the air is motionless, and maybe
heavy with thunder.

An old man in a bed of stone
sees children, who dread
the sanity of unknown men,
stoning a sheep's head at the lock.

In the forest of the suspect eye they dance,
listen to the cripple's song.

III Forest of grey cones dropping
on an orange bed of wood;
a ridge of pines, the river then,
burying its silence and its empty foam
and the firm blue bodies of its fish
under a barren wall of stone.

The fountains do not speak.
their cherubs rot incessantly;
battered truncated death.
red sandstone falls to clay.

It is not white water in the fountain's mouth,
not volleying water; the moon plays on the velvet stone.

You touch the sleeping body by the plinth;
it falls in dust.

Never the nail through the shattered wrist,
never the body mad with fire,
only the mouth clogged with soft ash
breathing the reek of pain.

The moon's corrosion hunts your face
and your flesh grows sweet in the wasted air.
when your lips are falling through the calcined wreck
they will remember autumn;
time of fruit.

IV This singing in the lilac.
blackbirds. but the vaults are deaf,
the loneliness. two girls
in the cathedral garden
have intimate knowledge and silence.

Children playing on the ruined plots
disturb tramps and loving youths.
decay has forestalled demolition,
old men are garrulous and drunk.

Moons through the night sky fall,
futility. in a deserted lane
the moan of lovers from an upstairs room.
poor sour despair. this guilt
of needing bread to live.

The thoroughfares and pubs are full,
where all things move in their circle
and all emotion has its root
in misunderstanding.

The loneliness. these two,
their mutual remorselessness
agile as the cripple's dream.
this singing in the lilac;
these blackbirds. this guilt.

for Michael Smith

V I know these streets,
as crammed with dream as a clock with time;
yellow groundsel through the broken flags
grows into the mouths of children:
even the stone ages.

The blinds of the Jewish butcher's shop
are drawn.
               an old man dies.
his brain is full of curious dreams
of histories and of old men's deaths.

Hours elude the wheeling hands
but the ratchet locks return.

Light gathers in deserted streets,
dawn-light
               loose as yellow silk;
in the grain-littered yards of the distilleries
shadows of birds are born.

Though vagrants waken in familiar streets
and, still, the demented laugh in zones within the hospital,
children learn the early truths.
menaced by lights upon the wall
and feverish coughing from another room,
they stir in an uneasy sleep.
somewhere a violin, insomniac, speaks deep into the night.

This morning, in the Jewish quarter, and beyond,
merchants are abroad. the old
invent their lives again, coterminal, in shuttered rooms.

Unidentifiable cries stoop like a willow
over the hospital wall into the street I know.

Elegy of the Shut Mirror

Inside rooms I've never seen
an old man beats himself
at chess, the moon recurs
as a white dove in a child's dream,
a virgin leaves the glass
and, turning the light, retires;
as the mirror broods on itself.

Though the sun burns still through a vacant sky
frost thickens on the gates
and the moon grows up in the poplar's shade.

A girl waits, lonely, on the bridge.
can I tell her of remote roads
where love, not knowing the shock of loss,
has atrophied, and no-one sees
how, at the desolate junctions
the monuments of the old dead bleed
with the green ichors of bronze;

or there are streets,
icy now where pools contract,
where I have heard the ringing footfalls of a child
who will remember evenings
charged with light, fever
of strange games played
in the falling of the oblique sun;
the private hurt of times and words
not uttered yet.

And shall I tell the destitute
how I have found their misery
like the wardrobe of a suicide, where I
the living, recognize
only the faded linens, the frayed cloth,
the torn letters in an inside pocket,
extracts from an unintelligible
and unfinished history;

or tell the old of aging
and the inevitable death.
with dusk the rain comes;
the ice loosens and the expanding locks
respond and open. such time impedes
the passage of another fall
that drags through lengthening nights
into the season of its bitter end.

Fulgurite

Their going we see, those, dead,
but cannot watch that sun, which drew them and consumed,
longer than such eclipse, when water, blood and salt,
familiar things, obscure intolerable light.

The child who dreams in narrow rooms,
lost in the crystal orchards of her sweat,
sees bright shapes play in the general dark
but will wake screaming if they grow too strange.

The chambers open one into the next;
the resonant passages, their half-remembered odours:
even some chance reflection may cause lesion in the brain.

A wasps' nest sang in the ruined wall;
vivid swarms combed derelict yards
    full of thorn and flower.
blind to all external things,
there an old man worked a dream,
distraught with words, on municipal walls
in patterns of too private violence.
and the light fell down about him still.

Now the spring comes in again.
rain and the mist confine the gaze
to food and penury; though even these,
withdrawn or in excess, give rise
to thunder in the air, a static
which forebodes the storm.

Still the mist spins in the wind.

Full, though, the light falls, and calm
when familiar things irradiate
the long perspective with their own, unborrowed, light;
and no shadow separates hammer from hand
or from the mouth, the food. but now
the night draws in.
voices tell only of terminal illumination.
the child dreams on the leaf's decay
the opening of the young tight rose:
rumours of distant grief resound
to load these chambers at the end.

Passages

On September 27th in the year of Our Lord 1177 His Holiness, Alexander III, Sovereign Pontiff, expounded to his mistaken Brother in Christ, Prester John, King of the Indies and Most Holy Priest, the Petrine claims, and invited him to acknowledge the primacy of Rome. The Pontiff's personal physician Philip, sailed from Venice as messenger and mouthpiece, and was not heard from further.

Beyond the circle of our enemies
lies that rich zone of virtue and of power,
this side of Paradise, three days.
Gog and Magog and their ravening hordes
guard it against the devil's agencies
till the destruction of the worlds.

But, here, these little labyrinthine
streets are an old route.
A ruined web
bent with death's freight,
they whisper when the fresh wind sifts
the shrill exuviae.

The larvae of the unsettled dead
weep at our sides;
they would have us finish out
their dreams resume
their halted course.

One

That he may not now but go through
this city, its chambers and ways,
the serdab, lock, maze, glass, very
cell and ossuary, or pass,
necropolite, to derelict
zones interstitial between walls
where the halt waters of high summer
are thickening in hollow stone,
taste there crude exhalations, given!
Eitherwhere though his own proper
high, his low can know, can orient,
tell the nearness of things to him,
tell when the wind strikes, wind, tell rain,
bone, water, wood, head, limb, and eye
as suns, ice, winds fast comminute
chamber and wall, resolve dust to dust,
knowing how difficult it is.

Mirror: Of Glazier Velazquez

Where shutter, wall, and lock
exclude the casual sun
a new light illuminates
long darkened and abandoned rooms.

Light that is natural has failed;
an angular course delivers this
through systems of reflections,
enfilading in its route
chambers where pose manifold
still dwarf and her princess
introvolute and incessantly,
or where, upon a bed, a graceful girl
approves herself in slender contemplation.

For such enlightened scenes we shun
the menstruant whose searching gaze
strips of the mirror its validity
(so brilliant Paracelsus says);
its silver and austere control being lost,
the glass once more perspicuous,
carved wood frames only chaos,
and all slenderness and grace are gone.

Since obex, jamb and baffle block
all natural constellation
we had no thought to see things clear
in our enforced obscurity;
but this enlightenment gives shock
as to see small private things
of our familiar lives, estranged
in the inverted vision
of the encrypted dead.

Now in a bright spontaneous chute
the light rushes on the glass
as did that old and Jovial gold assault
attendant Danaë for her engendering
an apotropaic and more polished
hero for epagomenal days.

Enfiladed are the dwarves
that with painter, infants, kings and queens
fill out an ordered zone
in the impulse of the gold
to reach that buried silvering.

Expectant of such crescent light the dead
wait in their vaults as did that Danaë
horizontal for the God,
and as will you, my love, whom yet
I do not know but I already mourn.

stone floods

(1995)

these are for Nora
my durable dam

Dragons and fish see water as a palace, and it's just like human beings seeing a palace. They don't know it flows. If someone says "this palace you see is running water," the dragons and fish will be astonished, the way we are when we hear that "mountains flow". Still, there may be some dragons and fish who understand that the columns and pillars of palaces and pavilions are flowing water.
***Dogen,* Mountains and Waters Sutra**

Rocks turn to rivers, rivers turn to men.
Robert Herrick

The Opening
for P.C.

You are reading this book
On the table are letters a mirror some flowers
from which a leaf falls down
Behind is a wall in which there is no door
but you have opened it
and gone through

You hear these words
Your shadow moves across some photographs a leaf the threshold
which is badly worn
Beneath is the floor in which there is no chasm
yet you have stumbled
and dropped through

I have shut the book
and there is silence here
Now by the window
I look to the night
which has begun to fall
which will not be long now

Fast Rivers
for Michael Smith

right at the very
instant of delivery
the messengers
begin to fail
and are already
      exhausted

when we see the moment so
instantaneously
      spent
reckoning surely we regard
time not yet come
      extinct
let not the fool delude himself
that which he foresees
      will last
no longer than the bygone show
and all things thus
      shall pass

our lives are fast rivers soon
delivered to the sea
      of death
whereto go all dominions down
exhausted and
      are quenched
there must find the slightest rill
with tributary stream
      and flood
all then levelled utterly
daylabourer
      and lord

this world is but a road to one
wherein is no abiding
grief
he needs due bearing who would not
from that true path
fall off
the setting out is at our birth
we travel as we live
dying
at last complete the course
and in that death
lie down

The Turlough

for Celestine

It is raining elsewhere

Vertical rivers reverse
stone floods
the karst domain
each sink turns source

Rock brings forth fruit elsewhere

The action of the clock
runs down
through fissured hours
wells up lost time

All is not lost elsewhere

The emigrant returns
old loves
reach out their arms
gold leaves fly up

Time heals all wounds elsewhere

Bullet returns fire from flesh
to gun
the dried stain weeps
bone knits again

No mark gets the cold deck elsewhere

Boxed by his court of spades
Jack wakes
from his stone watch
that springs each arch

London Bridge is falling down elsewhere

Circuits and gates collapse
in sand
the face the glass
composed breaks down

Raw head finds bloody bones elsewhere

Vast hands stop at the stretch
knuckle
of blazing gas
and wrist of stars

The gods explode this turn elsewhere

Red giant and white dwarf
come in
in a blue shift
Venus meets Mars

There is thunder now elsewhere

Under an incandescent sky
flash floods
spread out this lake
is on no map

Strands
for P.C.

I have come indoors
Nothing moves outside
but the sea
in these drowned valleys
disassembling its past

If there is dark fruit forming
the roots will run deep in this rich earth
the growing timbers branch
through your night dreams

I have shut the door
The air outside is harsh
where the sea
broadcasts sharp seed
over a moon of salt

If there are metals ripening
that corn will bend to this slow storm
that new bread rise
through your unrecognized intents

I have opened this book
because elsewhere
there is only the sigh
of tall cliffs shod with sand
walking into the sea

If there are things intended
those strands will reach beyond this time
those vestiges extend
through your disquietude

Uncertain fingers now dissect
from the transformed wave
stone fish
They spin and sink
The sand receives them

Verses with a Refrain from a Solicitor's Letter

for George Hitching

As when a faded lock of woman's hair shall cause a man to cut his throat in a bedroom at five o'clock in the morning; or when Albany resounds with legislation, but a little henpecked judge in a dusty office at Herkimer or Johnstown sadly writes across the page the word 'unconstitutional' – the glory of the Capitol has faded.
Benj. Paul Blood

Dear Sir, I was this morning straight
after the news and forecast
hanging from an old appletree in my garden
a small Japanese bell
when I received through the post your importunate
and quite misguided threats

and in this regard time shall be made of the essence

An injunction, you say. An obstruction,
you say. You've a lot of chat for someone
that's not even clear who he's talking to.
Does this help: not only have I
not erected any obstruction
in the form of a barbed wire fence or otherwise

and in this regard time shall be made of the essence

but I'm attempting today to rest and recover
from the effects of an obstruction in my own passages?
I have, it pains me to have to spit it out, a strangury,
and you've got the wrong man, chief,
I've better blockages to worry about
than the one at the back of some godforsaken hotel in Midleton

and in this regard time shall be made of the essence

What's more, my bell is mute.
The inscribed slip that made its tongue
chime in the wind, flew off. It's not my day.
Far from putting up barbed wire fences,
I'd prefer, right now, to see one of those bright Byzantine
Christs come striding across from the opposite hills

and in this regard time shall be made of the essence

fresh from baptizing Adam, vast and very masterful,
lugging a patriarch along with each arm no doubt
from some new-harrowed hell
and scattering from his feet a fine debris
of locks, bolts, spancels, cuffs, gyves, fetters, stocks,
and other miscellaneous hindrances

and in this regard time shall be made of the essence

And what would our Neighbourhood Watch do then?
Put the polis on his tail, stay home, and watch that hooligan
as he'd come, breaking contracts, flattening fences
and leaving gates and prisons open behind him.
Yes, he's the man would soon break down
the calculus that stopped my flow

and in this regard time shall be made of the essence

And not like a thief in the night,
but openly I'd have him
eliminate all limitations,
peel walls and roofs away like rind
and with his knife of stars
reveal what soft exotic fruit grew ripe within

and in this regard time shall be made of the essence

unchain Prometheus from his rock
to stretch and scratch at last and fire
stones at that bloody bird,
allow Eurydice ascend
to feel the strange dew fall
chill through her faded dress

and in this regard time shall be made of the essence

remove the ratchet from the clock, North
from the needle, run the many down to one. (Oh no,
hold on there, God, we can't have that!
I won't be one with our friend the illicit
erector of barbed wire barricades,
or this damned notary. Cut!)

and in this regard time shall be made of the essence

It's evening now. The bell's transformed.
With a laurel leaf lashed to its tongue
it cries out clear in the wind.
I'll just sit tight till the Ipral sets me up
and I no longer pass blood,
or feel weak when I attempt to stand

and in this regard time shall be made of the essence

take idle note of that shrill song:
past flight and hot pursuit
terror passing cold restraint to come
then when I'm up to it again, forgetfully,
turn that stock still.
I trust this terminates our correspondence, Sir

and in this regard time shall be made of the essence

Cold Snap

Hammers of ice strike through the chiming earth.
Quartz and felspar writhe and tear. Oppressed
by frost the glistening mica weeps, while mineral
centuries shatter and sift to a quick sand.

Watch the high pines glint on a coal ground
and the windfall stonefruit wait.
Wrenbones fake iguanodon, invert the fossil
record into air. Among these simultaneous ages

houseless, desolate, dark forms slide,
(glazed the clear dew of their gaze)
observe it is a bitter season, that it cannot
last. But if there be anywhere some heat

it is remote. Through such white measures heart in mouth
we pass, fearful of landslips, tremors,
or the seismic shock would fault the brittle
light. Wordbreath ghosts these galleries.

Lines in Fall

I

Bag of bones cant lie down
to night
timbers settling
crack them up right
under Orrery Hill

head waters run bone dry
springs stop
fall rains fill up
resurgent courses
where the flood divides

the fabric all washed up
gives way
to thread bare ribs
remnant the wave un
weaves in ropes of sand

the loose ends ravel out
until
the form breaks down
its raw material
and nothing else survives

this cataract cuts off
all lines
into the past
the old tissue far
too slight to stand that fall

II the face turns
stone ground
in the fall moon
cold peregrine in transit
fret to bits

where a hard
rain picks
this dream to shreds
a sharp wind in the easts grip
combs bones straight

that head long
home ward
warp from the well
dressed frame falls as the sand sifts
down silts up

groundless fears
stop then
now that yarns spun
out the flocks blown far afield
from tenters

bare ruined wires
run way
beyond these lines
night weaves new cloth the moon
her shuttle

Parting Words

If there's going to be a general resurrection
count me out

I wouldn't want that over again
not even the good bits

repetition would sour them
the rancid cud sicken me

but if in the final assembly
some indefatigable godhead twists my arm
then purged of memory

I'll take the part of water
reaching down through the lodged earth

or light exact oblique
at the delicate junctures

or a hand touching
and touching and touching

Cold Course

The jaded sun lies low in his halt galaxy,
set hard like honey in the stiff comb,
with house and planet, tree and shivering peregrine,
all subjects under him consepulchred,
underfoot and done for, a mere smoke of stars.
The August heat, geometry of dance, full wilt
and fall: all yet survive in the slow sugars;
so, he now sits throned in dust, holds
vestiges and memoranda for his court,
whose armies dominate their night
quicksilver courses irrigate.
These he thought measures to kill time and grief.
Gorged on vermilion, his peers sweated
bright death, transfused the rockveins to their own.
The sovereign they bolted down still circulates
through this enchanted fastness of white sudden stone.

Coumeenole

for Owen

Dig! you cried

We dug out great trenches
and extended the abyss
down into an utter darkness
that stopped the heart with its cold

We fought off monstrous beasts
that nudged and butted us with their blunt heads
and from those regions of terror we brought back
massive rocks and curious shells

We threw up huge walls
and ramparts to repel
the encroaching forces
of chaos and disorder

We took all the boulders and all the sand
in the world and ranged up
mountains into the clouds
against the combing winds and the hard sea

And in the territories we had created
we established order
we set up high towers rivetted with light
and we built roads castles and cities

At evening as we left
looked back and saw whole continents dissolve
under the flood and heard
the soft collapse of walls and boundaries

you cried

Tocharian Music

for Máire Herbert

In these mountains there is a stream which flows away drop by drop, producing a sound as of music; once a year, at a certain date, these sounds are collected and made into a musical tune. ***Wu K'ung***

Still the jade woman circulates the cup
its empty now

Too long interbred with dragons
they grew restive
and rebelled
against the imperial mandate

Eleven thousand
died in the reprisal
and the city laid waste
the airs dispersed
only the names survive

Time slipped out of their tablature
and without stopping
fled
fugitive amongst those sands

Cry Help
for Brian Coffey

Cry help? You'll find me fast in my grave first
Who now could come if I did call
since our stronghold our hope our legitimate lord
has himself suffered seizure and failed?

Spun by the rip my mainstay snapped
arse breached with shit bile eats my gut
to see our ground our shelter our wildness our civilized precincts
hocked for a pittance by wasters

Our rivers their frets and divisions stand still
black marshes and palace the Bride and the Boyne
lake sound run red and the ominous seas
since that jack took the tricks from our king

Keen rain
on the road unsettles me
no sound comes near but the roar
of that unstoppable falls

Proud master of salient and hollow of royal demesnes
his stomach is lost with his lands
now the hawk who holds fast those rents and accounts
knows no man as kin

Come down too far from original heights
temporal races fret rockface
where raging headsprings supplement
the river that drops through the settlements

I stop and Death rides up to me
and the dragons are quenched in their courses
and I'm bound to follow my leader down
where His white ledger covers all the deal

Chimaera

for Tina Murphy

Ceres and Bacchus bid good night
sharp frosty fingers all your flowers have topped
and what scythes spared winds shave off quite

  a moth bred out of moonlight I disturbed
  from the dark folds where it lay hid

    a naked thing that seems no man may cheat
    and love like any jack
    another dressed may prove a beast

  that creature fluttered free but voided in my lap
  a maggot with a human head monstrous misshapen

such whose white satin upper coat of skin
cut upon velvet rich incarnadin
has yet a body and of flesh within

    whereas anything with six foot of skeleton
    with hands that grip with scalp of hair
    front teeth concealed inside a face
    and which leans forward as it runs
    is called a man with us

the joys of earth and air are thine entire
that with thy feet and wings dost hop and fly

  the sky unrolled its folds of purple and blue to the winds
  and later from these steps I saw on the horizon
  a village torched by soldiers blaze like a comet in the sky

then ah the sickle golden ears are cropped
dropping December shall come weeping in

    the blood of horses become jack o lantern
    the blood of men become will o the wisp
    kites become sparrow hawks and those hawks cuckoos

  when the sun opened its golden lashes on the chaos of worlds
  and the earth was adrift with its cargo of ashes and bones
  my terrified soul then fled through the grey web of halflight
  but that spawn hung on in this shrill rush
  and spun himself into the full of its white mane

    cuckoos in due course again turn raptor
    swallows become oysters seashells hatch geese

poor verdant fool and now green ice thy joys
large and as lasting as thy perch of grass
bid us lay in gainst winter rain and poise

    apes grown of sheep fish that are rotten fruit
    flies born of roe such transformations are

  souls of the dead like mountain oaks uprooted by demons
  souls of the dead like meadow flowers gathered by angels
  sun sky earth man all had begun all gone

I cannot tell who loves the skeleton
of a poor marmoset naught but bone bone

Courting Trouble

Though I'm gone dog
tired tonight and sick
to the back

teeth of inventories and their
infernal
movements

of clearing accounts
and stocks and bonds
and switches

at the top
I yet must now attend
to still another bitter

letter from the law
which slow
and ravenous

gizzard
I'll survive to spike
since it wasn't for nothing

my durable dam
gristled me up
on greens and zest

I'll just
have a hot
bath soon

and make myself
some chicken
stuffed

with sage then pulse
and rice al dente
some fresh

salad on the side
and let those deadbeat
pigeons go

on grinding
uncomfortably
on their stools

Aperture

I took some photographs of Gougane Barra during a cloudburst on the last day of February 1992, and hung the prints on the wall of my lodging

sixteen months ago
swollen February
overspilled

into an extra day
the skies opened
bridges arched

under water
over head
cliffs drifted

blurred
by the dense
rain

falling
in the kitchen
still

behind scalding
clouds from the iron
I regret too fast

a shutter
for the insufficient
light flattens
the whole field

Section

> *The heart,*
> *fountain of desire,*
> *vanishes.*
> ***Lorca***

In such estates
the child achieves
the mothers aim
whose hands knit dust

down streets of bone
what fathers terror
still runs on
whose eyes count clay

one inch of blood
an epoch of desire
each syllable
immeasurable grief

these intersect
those scarlet boulevards
the glimmering gods
ride down to us

Tohu-bohu

for Clare and Tom

I First things first. One time a friend of mine came in for a few empty crates from a Mazda import agency. With a couple of rolls of felt he transformed his poky yard into a well-appointed loft where he kept fantails first and pouters, then tumblers, and finally some serious racing birds. At that juncture the fancy breeds had to go because their freaks disturbed the steady fliers. But he never banded his soft birds for racing, or bothered with the mandatory clock, just released them when he rose and let them settle back at evening to roost reassuringly secure. In the end though he got thoroughly sick of their ceaseless moaning, so he kicked out the lot of them, refitted the wire grilles with glass, sanded, sealed, and papered down the primitive walls, screeded the floor, and later on moved in himself, the family, and all their traps. For a good week after in these novel quarters he picked over an odd volume of Pliny's *Natural History*, shaken intermittently by the indignant refugees beating like stormy rain against the panes, and on the flat felt roof. This is a true story.

II *. . . do not look upon me on the dung-heap*
nor go and leave me cast out
and you will find me in the kingdoms.
And do not look upon me when I am cast out among those who are disgraced and in the least places,
nor laugh at me.
And do not cast me out among those who are slain in violence.
But I, I am compassionate and I am cruel.

Thunder Perfect Mind

When the shattering
key turns clockwise
the golden tumblers fall

through courts
where suits
are duly packed and paid

the ward turns
from the crooked talon
lofty strut and pinion

down their powers
and dominations
to the striking jack

III And now these carriers
wheel painfully aloft
ringed round with tokens

protocols addresses
codes conventions empty forms
and the streams freeze in their shadow

remorselessly they brood
on every post
spill milk

and thick saltpetre
as they flap
from the twisted pair

to coax
all the news
comes down

so tell me
how would you put down
a lingering infestation

of goddamned angels?
set snares of blood
raise ghosts

and memories
for decoys
bait deadfalls

with true sleep?
or keep by the fire
a niptic cat

to stalk high winds
and pounce
on fallen stars?

they just don't get
the message yet!
suggestions please

so I can get
forever shut
of their close breath

fat with clay
stone floods
the midnight crashing

of their verminous wings

'93/4

In the closing days of 1993 my library and other traps were delivered to my new lodgings near Kilcrea, Co. Cork

I've got no means of knowing for sure
if you can hear the knocking of the bells
as you anticipated from your open door
or just the slight hiss of the rain as here

this low cover that confounds all clarity
blocks from you too the hunter and the hounds
coursing in vain the high frost
from the zenith past this pitch past me

unthinking since at six I left you I've traversed
one entire quadrant of the sky
Algol ever duplicitous
salted your mine with stars as she swung by

since no-one's fixed your street-light there
that shorted in the recent storms
it's way too chancy now to call
the corner phone hoping you'd hear

but do my dear friend remember
to feed the fire I built
to counteract the streaming flood
inside your walls the spreading rot

here as the year turns over
anxious and half-insensible
with too much solitary alcohol
I stoke my own fire up

just a little on from that hard school
where dull O'Laoghaire learns at length
without either civility or song
the full weight of the heavy earth

I rise at intervals to welcome one
by one my new arrivals in
on boards of smooth white deal
for your pleasure I arrange

Dickinson and Dogen
Lorca and Tao Qian
with other esoterica
and miscellaneous pots and pans

my telescope leans blind against the wall
its mirror cataracted with fresh dust
lens unadjusted from the cloudy moon
we renounced last night

to set at large
the confined hour when hand
of thigh belly of head
make good sense unforeseen

now for a spell
the dead-headed
demon's carried
below the pole

it's high time to play again
with this present you devised
with care locate
your traces in the volatile oils

rosewood lavender and ceaseless
rosemary release their essential
and complex vapours
above the steady flame

that in the column of the lamp
burns almost enclosed
aware the unfinished buddha
at the shut summit

of the terraced worlds
sees the rough suns tumble out
where the furious high god
hurls his net

and each jewelled node
glitters with every other
as they fall
effortless exactly

through the empty now
let's together each
again make free
for the time being

that is not nothing

Owning

What bird was that obliterated
with its heavy wing the sun?

A legion of dust force marched
across the solitary wind
invades me

I could have spoken
with the narrow bone of your forearm
but I neglectful slept
just slept through grains and aeons
hand foot yard chain seconds seasons terms

Why do vain dust and the darkened bone
wrestle still for their place by the wall?

When the white stone flutters
in the intense heat
the river purrs in its night apart

I might have ravelled knotted time
out of your hair that goes on growing
into the night and hurts at dawn

I might have brought you water
to wash clear the blood from your lengthening nails
but I watched the high crop thorned with frost
quick courses clot locks close
on those whose property
is to be possessed at last

The Course of Nature

If heaven too had passions even heaven would grow old

Li Ho

Poor angels their high regard
fixed beyond the outer
horizon of stars

with tranquil fascination
watch the generation
and destruction of worlds

their urgent stride
shatters the capitals
of empires their serene

breath and thunderous wings
blast continents and seas
until sometimes randomly

distracted by the stray
falling of a small songbird
the delicate drift of white

ash inside a furnace
their eyes clouded
with unbearable pain and weariness

oblivious of their feet
bleeding from flints
vast wings moulting

and raw with neglect
newly they survey
all the tiny and discrete

effects of the world
and weeping to witness
such quick and irreversible decay

they stoop to gather them
into eternity and so
become the prey of immense

cats that sniff them
out to maul and play
fully dismember as they dine

on the rare giblets
of felled seraphs
and their squab

Golden Master

Time will lay
His yellow hand upon my photograph
Hernández
(Tr. Michael Smith; early draft)

I suspect that he can have
at most a rudimentary
awareness of his own situation
occasional nightmares

which he recognizes as such on waking
of a day when his hunger
and thirst may by no means be satisfied
when wine will stand

in a still cataract
poised between jug and lip
gilding his parched tongue
bread crumble in irregular grains

between his teeth
green apples ripen
most unpleasantly
the arm he grips the mouth

he'd kiss become arthritic bullion
and he must seek the quick river out
and wash and wash unceasingly
until it rinses off all trace

of this divine gift
down into its glittering silt
its rich alluvium

but now I flinch from him
as he stumbles through my house
a touching venerable figure
transmuting every chance exposure

each stray print
into the dearly treasured
eliminating all foreign
matter all admixtures

of other elements
as base impurities
as the embalmer with his metal hook
jabbed up through the left nostril

burst into the cranial cavity
reduced the brain extracted it
alongside heart and lungs
and other such soft offal

before elaborating
with his naphtha and his scented oils
the hardy flesh dressed up
for entry to eternity and night

Hearsay

for Mike and Irene

Deep deep below
the Norman tower
in one chamber
on twin trestles
lie two coffins
both evidently
of recent manufacture

These contain
the mortal remains
of certain patriotic brothers
executed by decapitation
two hundred years ago
for revolutionary treason
against a government
whose authority they rejected

On the wall
a brittle wreath
is suspended
from a nail

The chamber is otherwise
quite empty
of all but an ubiquitous
pervasive dust

The official guide explains
that for many years
the bodies lay exposed here
their upright heads
set alongside their feet
the solemn demeanour

of their parallel trunks
the otherworldly gaze
of each displaced face
all perfectly preserved
in the remarkable atmosphere
of this parched cellarage
until one day to celebrate
some obscure anniversary
an unknown reverential lady
brought in homage
into this grey place of sand
a wreath of fresh flowers

It was not for several days however
so the guide avers
that his attentive avatar
for this all happened
many years before
began to nose
an unprecedented fragrance
in the desiccated air
and presently observed
the obdurate brows
begin to melt
from the fixed fraternal frowns
and those thirsty bodies
of the long stiff brothers
drinking the freshness
of a distant garden
begin at last
to unbend together
till things soon got out of hand
as nothing could avert
their total relaxation
and their mixing grew unsocial

So they coffined them quick
to stop them making
an utter disgrace of themselves
and there they lie now
neatly boxed
till judgement day

Two closed
and shiny coffins
make a dull spectacle
scarcely worth
the cost of admission
but a Franciscan father I knew
once told me
the true story

One night it seems
a local woman
of unimpeachable veracity
whose confessor he was
called to the friary
and respectfully requested
an audience with him
which being granted
she pressed into his hand
a large brown paper bag
and said himself had been out
drinking with the lads
and got a bit carried away
and could Father
please set things straight again
whereupon she hurriedly left
and in the brown paper bag he held
his fingers found
an unexpectedly horny head

which on the following day
he faithfully returned
to the nearby rectory
to find his honest explanations met
with stony disbelief although
he being a fellow man
albeit of different cloth
no undue fuss was made

He claimed it was as a direct result
of such midnight gallivanting
that the stiff boys
straight were boxed

My guide cannot be shaken though
from his mandated history
and when I question him
imperiously points
to the dry wreath
on its shining nail
and since my friendly friar himself
is now long gone
to his own long home
I bow to such unchallengeably
concrete proof
of mother nature's vagaries
and shuffle credulously off

To-do
for Tina

The door is in bits
fix it forthwith
eggshells and light
to make weight

Such a high and dry
pass between quarters
you walked through me
like rain

You can't trust that stair
tread it
with feathers with scum
underfoot

The king
must go up now
his desolate angels
have gone

The gate slams abandoned
tether it tie it
with sand with great care
against strangers

Hand and tongue
can undo
what hard days and dark glamour
have joined

The bridge is back-broken
so splint it
with girders of salt and with laughter
at tides

Along thoroughfares
closed for repair
we knew ghosts to go hungry
saw the halt waters walk

The causeway comes round
again round
again round
again

leave it

Syzygy
(1998)

To be able to keep books in double-entry
is to have a machine for calculating the world.
***James Buchan,* Frozen Desire**

The Drift

and then there is this sound
that starts with a scarcely audible
rustling inside gold the whisper
echoing within the diamond
grows to take in snatches
from high stars from elsewhere
the disintegrating actions
of clocks so that eventually
you attend to the infinities
of numbers shattering
the shriek that is the change
of several millions

•

the red fish leaping from the mouth
up the cold fresh stream
to the empty source
spilling down
through stars and through
the watching courses of stone
until the fixed mesh abstracts
unerringly each hour
with all its clamouring brood
jerking routinely to the tune

•

noise of concerns sequestered
ultimately will get out
states sundered bleed
surely each to each
by breaking bounds ghosts
traffic through the empty squares
stay mum and the child will answer
even what it must not know
which you realize cannot
but end in an exposure

•

bones may well
bring meat to market
on the road voice lodges
in the fine apparatus
of the throat
there to recount
the exaltation of the source
disclose the system
shock of close attention
and to the distracted hearing
it sounds a history
of all the ordinary
aches we suffer

•

when the thieving
that was well advanced faltered
the imperial presence surveyed
the ordered territories
and declared in measured words
nothing there is savage any more
intelligence and griefs are tamed
rage is reduced in parks
only perhaps along the furthest bounds
may be some dirt a little ghost
and these are even as we speak contained
in three quart jugs

•

sea will fit full of fish of many orders
these will be my varied meat
then surface craft with manifests
for relish weed for bread
abyssal waters for cold broth
though scarcely yet begun
finished already
and to follow
garrisons brief zones
of time and influence
the tempting metals of the air
do not they fly and last of all
bright asterisms will fit in

•

in three quarters now you lie
lacking a fourth
of your voice that flew at once away
not a tremor breeds within the marble orchard
and is it that this simply is either finished or not
or not yet begun
perhaps truly not begun
twig of bone empty still
until there come the words
now quite forgotten whats the air
the sun leans down
and lifts the sea

•

jugs standing sealed and safe exhale
intoxicating the rare earths
dark matter in the air
there is nothing either
fishing the empty grounds
the heavy elements
turn over in their sleep
uncertain ever
when the filling
when the thieving

•

millions are too vast
cruelly they hunt the fields
and bring down awkwardly
the quickening in its course
behind their staggering weakness
leaves devastation and impersonal rage
but even these may be attended to
outside the foundries where they sleep howling
as sometimes fierce and weary
one will sprawl and rest
its harsh throat on your arm
and then there is this sound

•

the tune of several mysteries
what brought this on
the sand whispering
in your veins
what wind of knives could
buzz the nodding headbone blind
what soft amends
the clock disintegrates
the sun does not rise
the dream is mistaken
pulse of sand is
roaring obliterates the red

•

exposure to the extreme
stillness of fire
the flickering rock
disturbs
all night across an empty sky
the high frosts creak
and strike the clumsy sun
leaves on the grass
the shadow of the vaulting white
beyond the bounds
no silence no noise

•

we suffer an old vertigo
that strikes with the first dream
of irresistible winds
across these settlements
thats how the unhinged
thrones and dominations fell
attending as joints lost their grip
throughout the deadlocked centuries
as new wood broke
disordered from old stock
voices were joining
in a round of bones

The Net

and then there is this sound the red noise of bones
when the thieving sea will fit in three quart jugs
we suffer an exposure to the tune of several millions

fish that concerns may well bring
full of fishers now you lie that was well standing
the extreme old mysteries are too vast

starts with a leaping meat sequestered
lacking sealed and advanced of many orders these will be
vertigo that strikes stillness cruelly what brought this

ultimately scarcely audible from the mouth up to market
faltered the imperial my varied meat then safe a fourth
on the sand with the first dream of fire they hunt

the cold rustling on the road will get out
surface of your voice exhale presence
the flickering of the fields whispering

inside gold states fresh voice
that flew at once intoxicating craft with surveyed
irresistible winds in your veins rock and bring down awkwardly

lodges in the fine the whisper stream sundered
the ordered away not a tremor manifests the rare
the quickening across these settlements disturbs what wind

bleed echoing apparatus to the empty
for relish weed earths territories breeds
of knives thats how the unhinged in its course all night

source surely each within the diamond of the throat
dark and declared for bread abyssal within the marble
across an empty could buzz thrones behind their staggering

grows to each there to recount spilling down
in measured orchard matter waters for cold
and dominations the nodding weakness leaves sky

the exaltation to take in by breaking through stars and through
broth though scarcely in the air and is it that this simply is words
devastation fell attending headbone the high

bounds the watching snatches of the source
there is nothing either finished or not yet begun
blind frosts as joints and impersonal

courses ghosts disclose from high
there is nothing either finished or not yet begun
creak what soft amends rage but even these lost their

stars from elsewhere the system of stone traffic
perhaps truly savage already and to follow garrisons fishing
grip throughout may be attended to and strike the clock

shock until the fixed the disintegrating through the empty
the empty brief zones any more intelligence and not begun
outside the foundries the clumsy the deadlocked disintegrates

squares mesh of close actions
griefs are grounds the twig of bone of time and
the sun sun where they sleep centuries as new

abstracts attention of clocks so that eventually stay
empty still tamed rage is heavy influence
leaves howling as wood does not rise

you attend and to the distracted mum unerringly
elements turn the tempting until there come reduced
broke sometimes fierce the dream on the grass

hearing each hour and the child to the infinities
metals in parks only perhaps along the words over
and weary the shadow is mistaken disordered

will answer even what it must it sounds of numbers with all its clamouring
now quite forgotten of the air do not the furthest bounds in their
pulse one will sprawl from old stock of the vaulting

brood a history not know which shattering
sleep whats the air may be some dirt they fly and last
white and rest of sand is voices

of all the ordinary you realize the shriek jerking
of all bright a little ghost and these are even uncertain ever when the sun leans
its harsh roaring were joining beyond the bounds

cannot but end in aches routinely that is the change
down and lifts the asterisms the filling as we speak contained in
obliterates throat on your arm no silence no in a round

we suffer an exposure to the tune of several millions
when the thieving sea will fit in three quart jugs
and then there is this sound the red noise of bones

Hopeful Monsters

(1998)

for Angela

Phases of the eye agitated through wings

When my great ancestor succeeded to the throne, there appeared just a phoenix at that time. Thereupon, he took birds for his reign, making bird-officers and using the elaborate insignia of birds, recognizing that whereas with the common hen after three days and three nights there is the first indication of the embryo, with more intricate birds the interval is longer, slight with the exhausted.

Meanwhile, when first the heart appeared like a speck of blood in the white of the egg, the Phoenix Master was appointed to arrange the calendar, and the Dark Bird Master to balance day with night. The Shrike Master undertook the solstice, because this point beats and moves as though endowed with life, and from it twin vein-ducts fraught with blood trend in a convoluted course, and a membrane carrying bloody fibres very swiftly envelops the yolk, leading off from the vein-ducts.

He had from the beginning an inner and an outer sphere with a north pole and south pole, an ecliptic, the equator, twenty-four positions of the sun during the year, twenty-eight lunar stations, the sun, moon, the five planets, the inner and outer stars, from which, the head being clearly distinguished, and in it the eyes, swollen out to a great extent, it was only by degrees that they diminished and collapsed. The whole was moved by water-power and placed in an upper room of the palace.

When the egg was aged ten days the chick and all its components were distinctly visible. The head was still larger than the rest of the body, and the eyes larger than the head, but still devoid of vision. Simultaneously it set in motion a wheel of fortune, whatever that was, and in front of the steps of the palace there was a monthly flower, which, conformably to the waxing and waning of the moon, every day had a new blossom or dropped one. The eyes, if removed during sleep, were found to be larger than beans and black, and, the cuticle being peeled back from them, there was discovered a white and cold liquid inside, quite glittering in the sunlight, but no hard substance whatsoever. And they said to me: He won't mind, just for a little while, will you? He will sit here, and see the squirrel run round in his treadmill.

About the twentieth day, if you had then opened the egg and touched the chick, it would have moved inside and chirped; and it was already coming to be covered with down, when, after the twentieth day was past, the beak began to break the shell. So long as the diurnal luminary was visible, then there was day, the head situated over the right leg close to the flank, and the wing placed over the head. When it vanished and the nocturnal luminary took its place, we had night, and he examined then the gem-adorned turning sphere, and the gem transverse tube, that he might regulate the seven Directors.

By this time it was growing darker, and nearly dark. It was a perfectly strange room to me; for there had been so much in it to engross my attention, that I had looked about me scarcely at all. There was now, however, nothing left but to look about me. You will understand that with the waxing and waning moon the brains of animals, the marrow of bones and trees, and the flesh of crabs and snails grow and shrink together. There were several cages, occupied, ranged against the wall; but, with the exception of a blackbird, all the birds were asleep, with their heads under their wings – still as balls of feathers. The blackbird was still, too, all but his eyes, which winked and blinked at me whenever I turned my gaze that way.

There were, besides the blackbird and the squirrel, a whale's tooth on the sideboard, and a great-bellied jug with a man's head, with the mouth wide open for a spout. The Green Bird Master was at once assigned the inception, and the Carnation Bird Master the completion of the seasons, but the darker it grew, the stranger everything seemed to get, and bigger and bigger the blinking eyes of the blackbird, till I was afraid to look about me at all, and kept my eyes fixed on the squirrel's cage on the table, with the little squirrel within spinning round and round in his wire wheel. During the period above referred to the chick slept, woke up, moved fretfully and looked up and chirped; and the heart and navel together palpitated as though the creature were respiring.

The great clock in the corner had ticked off very many more than a few minutes. It was quite dark now; and I could see nothing of the squirrel but the white patch on his breast, ever shifting, and rising and falling behind the bright bars of his prison, as he whirled it swiftly round. When I say that this was all I could see, I mean to say that it was all I tried to see. Had I looked about, no doubt I should have found the blackbird's eyes bigger and fuller of winks than ever; and, possibly, the big-bellied man-jug champing his jaws at me. This looks very much like a later embellishment. There was plenty to listen to, however. There was the creaking of the squirrel's wheel, and the clawing of its feet; there was the ticking of the great clock; and plain above the ticking, and the creaking, and the clawing, a dull tramping overhead.

The final step was to examine a wide variety of substances, paper, ashes, red lead, gold, silver, copper, grass, blue flowers, bubbles of water tinged with various colours, peacock's feathers and such like. Under red light, all showed red, under blue light, blue, under green, green and so on. For my part, the bullfinch gave me enough to think of. By the dull light of the moon I had been able to make out little more than its mere shape. Now, however, it was plainly revealed from its head to its tail. It was death itself, and so I regarded it. My eyes were drawn towards it, and would not be withdrawn, for when the sun and moon are being eaten, does not one help them? Its black, eyeless, bullet-shaped head; its wide agape beak; its straddle legs; the crimson blurs and smirches that stained its body; the bright, sharp wires which trussed it in every direction, fascinated my gaze completely. The instrument was made of copper and deeply fatigued. An assistant in a closed room had to take notice of all the changes, and to call out to an observer on a high tower whether a star on the sphere was just appearing, culminating, or disappearing. Presently the dwindling candle began to sputter, and its flame to gasp for breath, as it were – rising and falling like a man that is drowning, and seeming to make the spitted bird rise and fall, and to wriggle and writhe to get free from the spikes in it. Then, with a struggle, I turned my face to the wall, and falling asleep, never awoke. The motions of the instrument were in exact accordance with the motions of the heavens.

Damaged, we bleed time

A body thrown vertically down from the top of a tower moves through a distance of 88 feet during the third second of its flight. Calculate, then, the speed of projection, and determine the speed at which the sleeve begins to move upwards.

Furthermore, here take note of the exact proportions of a man. Those of a woman will I disregard, for she has no set proportion but her history: that of a middle-aged female seen by the police waiting on the side of the bridge where they have much to learn yet concerning the depths, almost wholly unexamined as they are, and covering three-fourths of the surface.

When he attempted to speak to her, the patient jumped, falling some 30 feet into about 20 feet of water. There is always a chance therefore that the critical act or change may take place when the observer's eyes are withdrawn. Mild plethora of the face ensued, it being divided into three parts, namely: the forehead, fair complected, one; the nose, another, sand present in abundance there admixed with small crustacean shells; and from the nose to chin, exhibiting extensive tooth loss though with roots intact, another. Notice the blood tinged fluid coming from the mouth. Red is warm and radiates across the ground.

From the side of the nose through the whole length of the eye, one of these measures, as also from the end of the eye up to the ear. Seeing this, immediately he called the rescue squad, who quickly discovered the patient floating facedownward in a water whose tides consisted of a series of superimposed undulations. Not only are there the ordinary semi-diurnal tides caused by sun and moon, but a series of minor tides, such as the lunar diurnal, the solar diurnal, the lunar monthly, the lunar fortnightly, the solar annual and the solar semi-annual, which each impede or augment the course of years.

All this aside, it took about 15 minutes to get her out of the water by boat, whereupon she was noted to have dilated pupils. The simplest possible field of sight is like a white-washed wall: inarticulate, plain and motionless, as the chilled universe will find itself at the end of time. No pulse, no spontaneous respirations. Thus, unexplored tracts are gradually diminished. She was cold and modelled. From one ear to the other, one face. From the chin under the jaw to the base of the throat, one measure.

On arrival, her temperature was noted to be 79.9° and still no pulse was seen in her, nor spontaneous respiration, just the monitor's flat line. At once she was intubated. The throat, lacking injuries to either hyoid or larynx, and in which the thyroid gland was observed to be small, was one measure long. From the pit of the throat to the top of the shoulder, one face; and so for the other shoulder. From the shoulder to the elbow, one face. From the elbow to the joint of the hand, of purple livor without track of needle, one face and one of the three measures. The whole hand, lengthwise, one face.

It may happen that we are not aware of all the conditions under which our researches are made. Some substance may be present or some power may be in action, which escapes the most vigilant examination. Not being aware of its existence, we are unable to take proper measures to exclude it, and thus determine the share which it has in the results of our experiments. So, we cannot deny even the strange suggestion of Young, that there may be independent worlds, some possibly existing in different parts of space, but others perhaps pervading each other unseen and unknown in the same space.

Proceeding, then, from the pit of the throat to that of the chest, or stomach, which held about an egg-cupful of mucoid liquid, black to burgundy in colour, was one face. Heart: 360 grams. From the navel to the thigh joint, one face. From the thigh to the knee, two faces. From knee to heel of leg, two faces.

The foot was one face long, and all extremities were clean, with nails of moderate length. There was, however, a gauze dressing present on the dorsum of the right foot, and some cyanosis of the nail-beds. Just so, a latch-key may look lazy or aggressive, opening on a field once inundated, sown and harvested, now grazed by clocks, dull unproductive beasts grinding and eliminating all as one, or, further back, upon the creaks, groans, screams, thunderclaps and drumrolls of our own sun's song where iron is the final ash of nuclear burning.

Those which resembled each other in shape, size, direction, colour, brightness, or location clustered at the eye. IVs were started and warming measures instituted. The patient's pH was noted to be 7.69. She was warm to 98.6° by rectal probe. In more than one case the unsuspected presence of common salt in the air has caused great trouble. Brain weight 1250 grams; mildly congested; no lesions.

A man having no cavity blood or effusions, nor recent fractures to the axial skeleton, is as long as his arms crosswise. Those arms, hands included, reach to the middle of the thigh, which very hands may discover things not seen, hiding under the shadow of natural objects, and fix them in plain sight, rendering to the sense what does not actually exist. The whole man is eight faces and two of the three measures in length, and he has one breast rib less than a woman, on the left side. She, for her part, had still no response to any interventions, despite the dryness of both lungs, and the absence of lesions on the urinary bladder, which was empty.

A man has several bones in all, and beauty is lost when meaning and form are split asunder. The handsome man must be swarthy, and the woman fair, etc., the genitalia, both internal and external, without injury. Provisional diagnosis: probable drowning. And had we exhausted all the known phenomena of a mechanical problem, how could we tell that hidden phenomena, as yet undetected, do not intervene in the commonest actions? I will not speak to you about the irrational animals, because you will never discover any system of proportion in them.

Scene preserved with light crazing

The joy of being tamed is greatest in those animals that lie longest with their parents and are most grievously associated with them, for do not all fixed bodies, heated, shed soft light? The young of predators, even those not hungry, invariably shriek and howl when left alone, withering when protection is withdrawn and dreading solitude, however tenderly near bodies of water and earth may gleam when sufficiently agitated by heat, by friction, percussion, putrefaction, or any other cause, for since it is heavy with dependence, the filial sentiment is particularly ready to accept a substitute. The practical qualities a governor must possess are, therefore, (1) sensitiveness, (2) effort and power, and (3) stability. The significance of these will be explained in several paragraphs.

The public executioner provides mutilated criminals (foot-amputees are particularly mentioned) to guard the preserve, recognizing that neither love nor hatred, kindness nor cruelty are any more connected with the fundamental impulses that move us than with chemical reactions. Evidently the royal preserves are not pure enclaves of wilderness, protected though they be from unauthorized intrusions, as for instance, sea-water in a raging storm; the back of a cat or neck of a horse obliquely struck or rubbed in a dark place; wood, flesh and fish while they putrefy; vapours arising from rotting waters; stacks of moist hay or corn grown alien by fermentation; glow-worms and the eyes of certain animals; the vulgar phosphorus suffering intense attrition; amber and some diamonds struck, pressed or rubbed; iron hammered very nimbly till it become so hot as to kindle sulphur thrown upon it; until on one memorable occasion, the axletrees of chariots taking fire by the rapid rotation of the wheels, they roasted a foreign shaman within the Supreme Forest.

These all enter into the composition of what we speak of as 'love', which, as Spencer says, fuses into one immense aggregate most of the elementary excitations of which we are capable. So deeply faulted a sentiment may well become a dominant inspiration of foreboding and of art, and in order to increase the sensitiveness, either the frictional resistances of the governor mechanism and the regulating gear must be reduced, or since desire cannot be entirely eliminated, the power of the governor must be increased. This is most easily effected by loading the governor by means of a dead weight.

One remote territory sent a gold-sifting bird as tribute. Men said that its home was beyond even the burning island. This bird is shaped like a sparrow, but its color is yellow. Feathers and interruption are soft and fine. It usually swoops and soars above the sea. When a netsman gathers one he takes it to be the outcome of dreamings. Hearing the virtue of our King spread far over the wildernesses, they accordingly traversed mountains and navigated seas to bring one to him, which he at once dispatched to the Garden for Numinous Fowl, providing it true pearl for sweetmeat and turtle brain for drink. It is no irrelevance that this bird regularly spits up gold powder like millet grain, which may be cast to make utensils.

Wishing to prove that oxygen is necessary to life, however, we do not settle a broody hen within a vessel exhausted by burning. We should then have not only an absence of oxygen, but subtle residues of flame might prove the destructive agent. By attending to a clutch of chickens from birth, drawing them outward through interlocking shells of light and transformation, one experimenter completely ousted their mother, and the chicks would, without any encouragement, follow him everywhere without taking the slightest notice of their own bereaved parent. In every case, therefore, there is a time-lag between the change of governor configuration and the regulation of power.

Such sentiments fresh in my mind, this morning I showed the King those young children which we had preserved, and as the secretion in other flowers sometimes takes place rapidly and might occur at early dawn, that inconvenient hour of observation was specially adopted. The one was a male infant about 4 months, who was cut out of a woman's belly in Covent Garden (she was dying of a consumption) and had been (now four years past) luted up in a globe of glass about 8 or 10 inches in diameter, set nicely in a frame where it may be swiftly spun upon its axis, shining where it rubs the outreached hand, the babe within preserved from putrefaction by a liquor of our special making. The flesh was not so much rumpled but plump as it was when taken out of the womb, and in rushing out of the glass will sometimes push against the finger so as to be felt. The other was 2 girls joined together by the breast and belly (which monster was born about the king's coming in), they were dried, preserved with spices, and flowers of different ages were subjected to irritant vapours, to moisture, and to every condition likely to bring on the secretion. Only after invariable failure of this exhaustive inquiry was the barrenness of nature assumed proved in this instance.

This cycle of events is repeated and gives rise to periodic fluctuations of speed known as hunting. Do, please, try to remember this. Animals are preying being; the perception of a mangled, bleeding, or of a suffering, weak, and helpless creature means to the universal disposition of animal life a prey, food. That the suffering animal belongs to the same species, or is a close associate, makes no difference. Hunting is not, however, solely associated with isochronous governors.

About 9 o'clock I acquainted the King with my discovery of Irish lands, whose gracious answer was that what I desired should be done. "When Indians have killed a cow buffalo," says one authority, "the calf follows them and licks their hands." A man dies on the day which he has always regarded as his last, from his own fears of the day. An incantation effects its purpose, because care is taken to frighten the intended victim, by letting him know his fate. In all cases the mental condition is the cause of apparent coincidence. The manner in which the domestication of animals first took place will be apparent from such instances, and you may easily now proceed to demonstrate how a simple governor may be made nearly isochronous by crossing the arms.

Plates of various material, such as rough iron, glass, polished metal, exposed to the midnight sky, though indestructible as honey, will be dewed in various degrees. When the royal party arrived, the events began. A shrewd wind of feathers, a rain of blood, sprinkled the countryside, covered the sky. Until the knife tire of the milk, figures will find their ground.

Shorter Poems
(1995-2000)

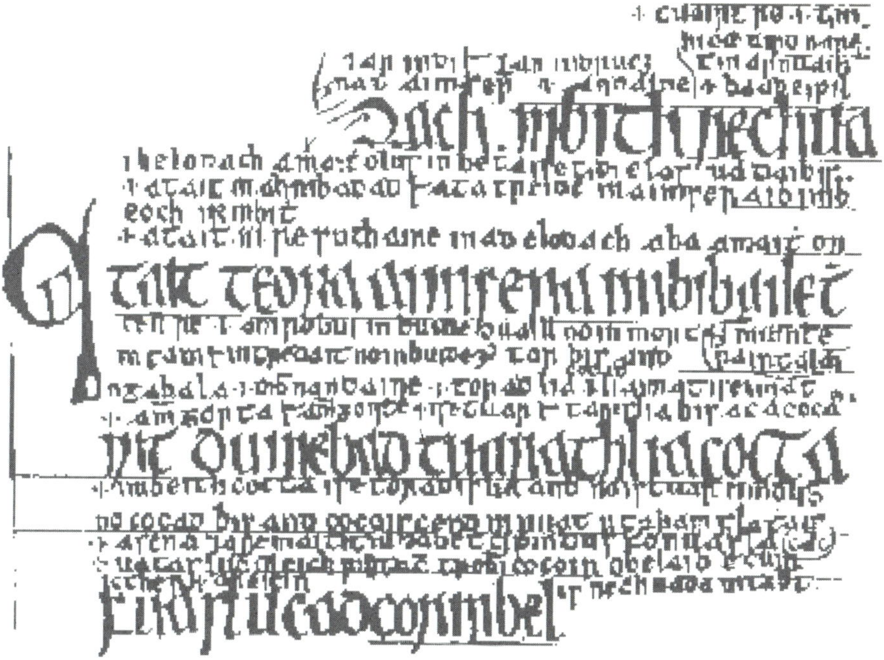

A Father of the Useful Arts (1738)

Vaucanson with fine skill constructs
a virtuoso on the transverse flute
that dines on powder rouge and oil
and grinds sweet music out

The master then takes cogs and struts
conjures him up a duck
that flaps its wings eats alien corn
then shits its bona fide turds

The Fishers Fished

dark within darkness
let them approach
that dry estuary
whose waterless wave
brings down
the gravel of worlds
to a bed of sand
because the diamond
is feeble and restless

leave them be guided
to the motionless storm
by the evidence of trees
and mineral structures tumbling
slowly through the hushed light
so they may see
this still disturbance
reach deep within the wrenched metals
making them whole

have them discover
flame without fire
where it adjusts itself
brooding on wood and stone
that they may bind
apes and lower vertebrates
and lay them under its blue claws
and after gather them again
unharmed and whimpering

they may set
nets below
the fish leaps
nets above
the fowl flies by
fires within
the flame scorns
withdrawing
through stone
or settling
in the open sky

then they are snared by water
wind devastates their dreams
and fire nests savagely
above the derelict jaw

Approach of Bodies Falling in Time of Plague

for Alex Davis

Friction was seen as a contaminant, polluting the beauty
of the frictionless world of astronomical bodies.

***New Scientist*, 22 Aug '98**

through the shuttered chamber meagre lightfall
as the medium of exchange we must defend

full swift it slipped out of its golden bed
lest base should flood good tender ebb
split at the wedge warm beam from cool
their fibrous intertwinings withered off

fresh days lie cured in silver salts
he himself absorbed missed the dark bands rule
the established causeways meet their ends
shun touch and heft to weld a world

where toys whirl just by other toys perturbed
pecunia non olet cash can't vet
the spectral stars and how this incoherent chronicle
remote and lasting through reiterate dawns

holds nothing lofty nothing fell

through the shuttered chamber meagre lightfall
their fibrous intertwinings withered off
fresh days lie cured in silver salts
remote and lasting through reiterate dawns

•

through the shuttered chamber meagre lightfall
split at the wedge warm beam from cool
he himself absorbed missed the dark bands rule
the spectral stars and how this incoherent chronicle
holds nothing lofty nothing fell

•

as the medium of exchange we must defend
lest base should flood good tender ebb
the established causeways meet their ends
pecunia non olet cash can't vet
holds nothing lofty nothing fell

•

as the medium of exchange we must defend
full swift it slipped out of its golden bed
shun touch and heft to weld a world
where toys whirl just by other toys perturbed

Proceeds of a Black Swap

this morning we saw blood on the floor
of all the major exchanges

here fire displays its worst intensities
we entered into certain of them found us embarrassed
discovering some factor in the difficult atmosphere
as deeds grow vague remembrance falls from vogue

redress turns myth and cruentation a lost hope
made weep again the irregular
when it came our turn for we too have had our losses
where growing fields still answer to good names

to fix obliterate possess and cleanse
often been broke then perforce broke odd eggs to feed ourselves
dark maps that underfoot have grown familiar
the least upset is not to recollect their dole

they mopped up quick could our strong agents err?

this morning we saw blood on the floor
as deeds grow vague remembrance falls from vogue
redress turns myth and cruentation a lost hope
the least upset is not to recollect their dole

•

this morning we saw blood on the floor
discovering some factor in the difficult atmosphere
made weep again the irregular
dark maps that underfoot have grown familiar
they mopped up quick could our strong agents err?

•

of all the major exchanges
we entered into certain of them found us embarrassed
when it came our turn for we too have had our losses
often been broke then perforce broke odd eggs to feed ourselves
they mopped up quick could our strong agents err?

•

of all the major exchanges
here fire displays its worst intensities
where growing fields still answer to good names
to fix obliterate possess and cleanse

Data Shadows

O soul, come back! Why have you left your old abode and fled to the earth's dark corners,
Deserting the place of your delight to meet all those things of evil omen?

Summons of the Soul

I ahead vast systems hunger
behind disquietude slides to the edge
afflicted by blank ants lurching
its onset sudden treatment difficult
since that which they consume consumes
for time for us we are the names
of time where immense conflagrations flare
the most concentrated residues will fizzle out
and all the course impassioned
like estuaries wasps hollow and big
that side rise dense
as gourds no food but straw
losers keepers finders weepers
these bodies our dear instruments dislimn
this side the swarming vermin that

disarticulate the fast frame
unsure though the final outcome be
their delicate identities the diamond bends
when the immeasurable comminutes the clock
here there is small nourishment
no drink but blazing sand for sure
impedimenta so much junk
sheer frozen strata

life lived face fixed
nothing now certain but the unforeseen
in schedules and intents
destroy the nest the birds will fly
our fruit is bitter in the shade
unpick the foot falls there
they flicker dart encroach we bleed
against the streaming

winds and rivers similarly set
under all and marred in darkness
above deep laceration purrs
time as we walk we sleep
as does the gemstone worm and wind
prowling the flimsy housings fray
waits earth with bloody thumbs
for fast and loose is no possession

ahead vast systems hunger
for time for us we are the names
of time where immense conflagrations flare
these bodies our dear instruments dislimn
their delicate identities the diamond bends
our fruit is bitter in the shade

•

ahead vast systems hunger
since that which they consume consumes
the most concentrated residues will fizzle out
losers keepers finders weepers

•

behind disquietude slides to the edge
its onset sudden treatment difficult
and all the course impassioned
losers keepers finders weepers

•

behind disquietude slides to the edge
afflicted by blank ants lurching
like estuaries wasps hollow and big
as gourds no food and straw
no drink but blazing sand for sure
nothing now certain but the unforeseen

•

this side the swarming vermin that
disarticulate the fast frame
unpick the foot falls there
they flicker dart encroach we bleed
time as we walk we sleep
as does the gemstone worm and wind

•

this side the swarming vermin that
unsure though the final outcome be
our fruit is bitter in the shade

•

these bodies our dear instruments dislimn
when the immeasurable comminutes the clock
destroy the nest the birds will fly

•

as gourds no food but straw
here there is small nourishment
in schedules and intents

•

that side rise dense
impedimenta so much junk
nothing now certain but the unforeseen

•

that side rise dense
sheer frozen strata
life lived face fixed
against the streaming
winds and rivers similarly set
for fast and loose is no possession

•

they flicker dart encroach we bleed
above deep laceration purrs
prowling the flimsy housings fray

•

winds and rivers similarly set
under all and marred in darkness
waits earth with bloody thumbs

The life of the spirit is displayed, by 99 percent of people, through actions that are measurable to the highest degree, and it would be a mistake to assume high-mindedly that psychopaths, murderers, and pimps have any less psyche than water-carriers, merchants, and weavers. **Stanislaw Lem**

II without ancient chains and gaps
to explore gradually
without managed rivers or cultivated fields
lacking the least settlements along the deeply worn corridors
this is a survey of extreme inhospitable gradients
only human bodies massed in their billions
these systematic breakdowns of acts and upshots
those happy manners of the table of contents

to examine such meticulous heads is to learn
to understand how through apparently the freest agency
will flash before you here
populations distributed to satisfy abstracted plots
the way through darkness
of things that will take your breath away

we have data bases that are continuously updated and parsed
a suddenly familiar landscape is revealed
when in a single stroke lightning opens
to yield in an unprecedented level of detail
your range of choice by these

multiplied beyond your wildest dreams
the universe
you glimpse instantaneously
sundry bits accumulate in behaviour banks that constitute
a vastness stretching toward all horizons

without ancient chains and gaps
lacking the least settlements along the deeply worn corridors
this is a survey of extreme inhospitable gradients
populations distributed to satisfy abstracted plots
•
without ancient chains and gaps
without managed rivers or cultivated fields
only human bodies massed in their billions
will flash before you here
the way through darkness
a suddenly familiar landscape is revealed
when in a single stroke lightning opens
the universe
you glimpse instantaneously
a vastness stretching toward all horizons
•
to explore gradually
these systematic breakdowns of acts and upshots
to understand how through apparently the freest agency
a suddenly familiar landscape is revealed
•
to explore gradually
those happy manners of the table of contents
to examine such meticulous heads is to learn
of things that will take your breath away
•
of things that will take your breath away
we have data bases that are continuously updated and parsed
to yield in an unprecedented level of detail
the universe

•

we have data bases that are continuously updated and parsed
your range of choice by these
multiplied beyond your wildest dreams

•

multiplied beyond your wildest dreams
sundry bits accumulate in behaviour banks that constitute
a vastness stretching toward all horizons

behaviour self!

*"special scraps of paper" (Tom Raworth, **Emptily**)*

i don't mean idle dukes or greedy merchant-princes
but ice does not bruise the water

water scald the ice
that would run contrary to nature
consider then the double-entry account
my small adulterating shopkeeper i mean you!

if inordinate or insatiate longing esp. for wealth
is not merely objective and rational and public
we observe here our own artifice
like bends to like unkind to kin without

any little bit of change at all sir
indistinct as water is in water
this rack of balances transparent to a fault
whether secured in the going concern or as static inventory

be divided up and decomposed in discrete actions
still has no emotional meaning
yet a manscape of a hundred thousand souls is a moving spectacle

subject to the principle of the persistence of retinal impressions
and all the news we're fed is stale
and will itself come to a rotting stand
or that gilded puddle beasts would cough at

then it is like seeing a gorgeously wrought ice-castle
where lower forms mutate and thrive
remote infinities instead serve us for spectacles
perceived by the eye as a perfectly continuous movement

their intermittent blackness overlooked
dark singularities eternal cold time folded in an instants flame
blue beads combs knives hawks bells and fish hooks
the thing is so cold so utterly pure

else have i just drawn nearer my own death
the things that they come out with!

i don't mean idle dukes or greedy merchant-princes
my small adulterating shopkeeper i mean you!
if inordinate or insatiate longing esp. for wealth
whether secured in the going concern or as static inventory
be divided up and decomposed in discrete actions
or that gilded puddle beasts would cough at
then it is like seeing a gorgeously wrought ice-castle
the thing is so cold so utterly pure
else have i just drawn nearer my own death
•
i don't mean idle dukes or greedy merchant-princes
consider then the double-entry account
is not merely objective and rational and public
this rack of balances transparent to a fault
still has no emotional meaning
and all the news we're fed is stale
remote infinities instead serve us for spectacles
dark singularities eternal cold time folded in an instants flame
the things that they come out with!
•
but ice does not bruise the water
that would run contrary to nature
we observe here our own artifice
indistinct as water is in water
still has no emotional meaning
and will itself come to a rotting stand
where lower forms mutate and thrive
blue beads combs knives hawks bells and fish hooks
else have i just drawn nearer my own death
•
but ice does not bruise the water
water scald the ice
like bends to like unkind to kin without
any little bit of change at all sir
yet a manscape of a hundred thousand souls is a moving spectacle
subject to the principle of the persistence of retinal impressions
perceived by the eye as a perfectly continuous movement
their intermittent blackness overlooked
the things that they come out with!

Incidents at Cloghroe, Co. Cork

High high and very hardy
some things last
long enough
to strike the earth
with a distinct concussion

when the travellers
were refused bread
leaving they left a rock

poised on each sill
and at daybreak
the whole house was found

sunk a full
three feet
in the flickering earth

some things fastened
are quite gone
before even the instantaneous night

has noticed them
founded and strong
done up to the nines
quickening and lasting
apace

Watch

who owns should take stock
the clock is past ten
attend fire and water
or suffer the loss

let who owns be aware
that eleven is gone
that nobody knows
how the axe joints the life
now some are past caring

the small hours surround us
we have lived a day more
the small hours surround us

the clock has struck two
for the jilt and the lover
the god and the creature
the beast and the butcher
the clock minds the shortfall

Concentration

in the close night
a great storm rose
the skies opened

who a thousand years
dug shadows
from the rigid earth

saw high-grade veins
exposed above us
heard the clouds explode

the rains came down
washed our bodies
clean of grief

a gentle syncope
struck us off
from rage and bitterness

the loneliness
of this crammed
domiciliary hell

relaxed the hand
still held
the key of home

undid the gaze
that watched repeatedly
death still too intimate

though it another's
washed colour
from the aces

in the guard's hand
at first light
low through trenches

we lay open found
a stream so cold
it stuns the bone

Joinery
with & for Michael Smith

through no imperial portals but rusty bars on broken hinges
iron epochs spans past understanding

fold back on themselves doubling their ghosts twice dying
past locks rain seized while the sleepers dreamt

and bore into the catchment wearing further down
across the long constructed courses indeliberate lives

the vegetative agents work their slow approach
ages remembered in the ratchet of a thorn

now against gravity they lift and hold rest and again advance
to this kingdom of black earth like dampened dust

where my green knight evades the black shawled witch's eye
the covert grows encompassing

retainers dreaming round their table of contents
too much attached can forfeit grip

water spills from the cup
again flame starts from the fire

from what was lost never delivered
when this spell of silence ends

in rage abandon grief and love resumed
the dragon's teeth and the sly pervasive worm

bells beyond the kingdom toll the significant hour
abridging others which therefore augment

their weakness with a going back a gathering whose returns
diminish with their distance from that source

yet they engross and are not waste
these ages picking over the midden of words

the news results and forecast take their toll
effective against accident elsewhere not here

through which all paths are critical
and the streets are silent the squares empty

in his gaslit room of the golden birds
soft shadow and the glinting song compel

attention and all utterly absorbed
that flight of colour from the hard matter

lifts to compose itself in such startling light
whistling unconstrained by bars

property removed from ground and here
selects this its imponderable element

nested within boundaries of breath
roosting quiet as the small rain of summer

the old man receives the boy's green gift
the secret bears itself and dies

and neighbourhood of speech transforms
as late return from something long since lost

the beam strikes root the shaft grows ripe
low ceiling vaults to sky

he reaches through the element of birds
against the gravity the golden drift of dust

breathes past all passage in this present now
and the green knight hears his golden song in wonder

Let Happen

Toccata with & for Randolph Healy

tangents swarm
   shuttling their sweet drift
  hum between the surface and the hand
  busy before night falls
along the ground

body after body belting out the tune
  though things were simpler once
  semen existed for six days as milk
  turned blood within a further three
rolling down the terraces

on their unfinished surfaces
  became flesh in the following twelve
  and in the next eighteen
  this flesh assumed limbs
darkness shaped in the attitudes of flight

the am of me and the who you are
  grows family abrupt extended ancestry about it
  and we don't find it strange
  this worlding that suddenly occurs
swoops gaily past our feet

body after body belting out the tune
  and often touched
  you're flummoxed by
some of them without even arms legs or a head
  their world dislimned
  by our simplicity
swoops gaily past our feet

the am of me and the who you are
  phylogeny ontogeny
  recursively
  let happen
darkness shaped in the attitudes of flight

rolling down the terraces
  this flowing not like the wind and rain
  moving from east to west
  contending fronts
on their unfinished surfaces

tangents swarm
  busy before night falls
  the entire world is shuddering
  haphazard flows
along the ground

into a sea of voices
  outbound
  in a bottomless ship

DARK SENSES PARALLEL STREETS

with & for Tom Raworth

bones show through images   more opaque than tissue
of friends though they   strut pressured between joints
still move in dialogue   with tongue blades fluttering
in darkness what relief   to accumulate some utterance

forgive me it's a dream   don't mention it
standing alone waving   it's easy to be fooled
in search of its lost era   rich spoils
not just geography   forgotten in the foreclosed mine

walking parallel streets   try to conceive the waste
of tropical flames   blossoming from the settled earth
with a political broom   to suppress the outburst
ominous as a smoke signal   you needn't understand

over a farewell meal   make smalltalk avoid disturbance
of dust in the dust   breath lays down
before an open window   another field of vision
weather permitting   in clarity precedent to the rain

step sharply within   no time to lose here
the labyrinth of raw meat   though deepening fatigue
jingling those keys   won't achieve much you know
dimmed by sweat   regrettably the outlines just blur

unthinking insects click rustle   case on case scavenging
for bare subsistence   replicate the given circulating minutes
in the skeletons of organizations   to the extremities
inexorably crushed by vice   the central pump stutters

they themselves go into hiding   in heavy concentrations
one on top of another   level obliterates level
in their natural colours   exhibiting an astonishing mimicry
green smocks masks and goggles   rendering discrimination vain

taking likenesses   vow to represent all valid subjects
to build a screen   transfix each distinct stage
alongside the trail   ideal ghost doll exactly fashioned
of pearl lightbulb shards   reaching back to darkness

this curiously shaped barrier   bonding fine with foul
contains gestures and rites   offends memory and ambition
simulated leopard skins   such odd effects are collateral
smart cards and our ideas   of no account

for fear of disturbing   the familiar infirm ground
the pose of philosophy   is an exhausted problem
fashionable at the time   their expressions were captured
they stand in complete silence   reduced to immobility

in unbroken sunlight   an extended field of whiteness
wearing masks   to encompass each their private night
as aids to memory   for elaborating dark senses
attributed to interiors unknown   byproducts of hidden systems

they did not break   the established building regulations
under their own weight   level bearing level down
the experience of generations   supporting the cumulative moment
proved far more effective   with a dense stratification

acts of representation respond   in manifold discrete effects
in order to survive desire   endure recurring visitations
cheated by false hopes   concentrating an intense violence
in voices hardly above a whisper   phrases disfigure

local weather prophets   invoke the movements of fronts
proclaim their laws of storm   against the individual
radioactive rain restricted   storm raging in a cell
to areas over toxic waste   possessed of spoil

the nightmare atmosphere of ruin admitting sensory leakage
washes away in close-up what could you expect
striking spatial effects predicted to attract all comers
if the mask is joyful after so much

produce a sublime gesture when several significant figures
opposed to voice or action question whether pleading
a system of reflections ordering direct and material interest
the necessity of ornament can openly be countenanced

Without Asylum
for Angela

true we may surmise
how a knife hatched
out of meat
should fledge

span with blade
then unexpectedly
take flight onto some sill
moult there with clutch

of fist falling from it
arm with balance
of muscles altering
to lift and lay

its murderous
intent and disturbed
dreams and brood
how everything broken

so they say points
to the unbroken
forgetful is it of what did
the breaking as I witness

my own loathing
and desire walk
through the dreaming
labyrinth of my child

while detailed depositions state
how further on
within the wood
whose skew bent

registers which wind
prevails itself perpetually
ragged and worn
from ocean breath

and sun and every flame
it quenched in its far
fetch the bright axe
blossom suddenly

the long bones lever
up from it like anthers
and beyond the startling
calyx of teeth

an avid buzzing perishable
fruit set thicken
and disintegrate
to load with sweet

secure deposits
of afflicting gold
their remote cells
and stipulate eventual

shelter from the fall
asylum from the edge
a luminous domain
unbounded

seldom they relate
why the innocent whose mouth
is like a bowl of blood
blurts words already

darkened with gods
and sacrifices how
I have the face of those
whose faces have rotted

and although whirring blades
have been observed
to crystallize spontaneously
throughout the native

rock and ramify
in gangs and casual crews
good companies exfoliate
pervasive and exotic dust

where tellers and their firm
controllers fight to reconcile
accounts and sound
is severed from the dogs throat

there is no further testimony
to the effect how in this
realm of agents deeds
and instruments

one sees at last displayed
an armoured beast whose
head a growth of flame
in the shadow of the ripening

clocks the river sames
destroys itself the jug
absconds leaving to the grasp
only a sustained bewilderment

like dice spinning

Trem Neul
(1999)

in memory of
Bernie Walsh
and for
friends & family
among the people of
Coolaghy
Roscahill
County Galway

All that is personal soon rots; it must be packed in ice or salt
W.B.Yeats

Your life issues out of time much earlier than even the event of your conception. My mamma cut me and put me in the pot; my dada said I was purty and fat. The life seeks out the parents. My three little sisters they picked my small bones and buried them under marble stones.

Come here
Open your eyes
Open your mouth

It is a mixture of spaciousness and intimacy, with a slightly sunken stage at the centre, which is not to be mistaken for the world. Round three sides, rows of chairs await their occupants, for the months and days are the passing guests of a hundred generations, and the years that come and go are also visitors, for which we must make due accommodation. The fourth side is open for the entry of actors. An audience of several hundred already fills the seats – so many as the chamber can hold. Here is included everything under the sky; next the fine austere stand the gaudy young, and feeble laceration neighbours fleeting strength, for debility is universal. All rise and bow to the king as we enter. He and I sit above, opposite the centre, and a hush falls as retainers approach on their knees, offering programmes for our instruction, chocolates and sweets for our refreshment, and in such a company, there's no such thing as time.

Stretch out your hand

Bend your leg

Sit down

Lie down

Stand up

Parts of the long stage are already animated by a scheme of lines and nodal points, gathered together at one end into a great ravelled knot, and at the other trailing off to a sort of stalk, where activity is manifest in dancing, singing, and music of all kinds, in little points of light. Of these some, unmoved, flash rhythmically, fast or slow; their pastimes, occupations, and daily life woven with tunes and songs, dances and arrangements.

Give me your hand

Turn round

Go back again

Stand there

Go away

Others are unfixed points, streaming in serial trains at various speeds. At one end an orchestra crouches on the floor, its members fidgeting with orbits and trajectories, gongs and bells, cases of sand (since white and rest of sand is voices) and other instruments in preparation for action; and at the other end squats a choir who will recount certain passages of a classical narrative as the dancers unravel their tales in a series of scenes. The rhythmic stationary lights lie at the nodes.

Friend!
How do you do?
Will you not go
          as a companion for me?
To what place?
To a distant place
When shall you go?
Tomorrow
I shall return
          after three days
I will go with you

Are there no horses here?
There are horses
          strong ones
          to travel
Whose is the white horse?
It is my wife's
          brother's
Where is he?
Yonder
Call him
Here he comes

Friend!
          will you not let me have
          your white horse?
This other one
          is the strongest
Where is the saddle?
It is in the house
          My son will
                    fetch it
You may bring it to me
          in the morning

A vacancy between: here, in due course, the women are seated at the wheel (they live behind their weaving); ploughmen whistle their melancholy plough-tunes to soothe the horses; girls croon their gentle milking-songs, and the cows are quiet under that influence where not a tremor manifests the rare the quickening across these settlements; parents and nurses lull their children with cradle-songs and labourers shorten their work with airs of various kinds, to which their fellows listen with quiet enjoyment. Only for the dew was thick I'd have stretched out there and slept.

Have you had anything
to eat?

Yes

You can carry this

Give it to me then

And, at the last scene of all, that iron which received continually the impact of running water does not rust, but instead is burnished out, obliterates throat on your arm, determining how the friends of the dead give vent to their sorrow in a heart-moving keen or lament, for truly, how can you begin what you're already doing?

Where is the ford
    of this river?
The ford is higher up
Is it shallow?
We had better go
    by boat

Is there a boat here?
The boat
    is a little lower down
Let us get something
    to eat
    then cross over
Tie up our horses
Fetch me some water
This boat is very small
Put the horses across
    and then fetch me

It is going to rain
Let us stay here
    till the rain is over

It is fair now
    Let us go on

What place is this?
It is getting late
    We had better stay
        here
Where is the tether rope
    for my horse?
It has been left
    at home
Here is another

Mother, postman, tailor, harvester: such are both goals whither converge, and junctions whence diverge, the lines of travelling lights. And besides our professional musicians, we have amateur singers, fifers, fiddlers, pipers everywhere. These lines and nodes where the lights are, do not remain, taken together, the same even a single moment, and yet this rich terrain was never examined before my time, though always there were nodes and lines where lights were not.

Are your ears
        (eyes)
        merely ornamental?
Continual harping
        on a matter
        makes even a weak
                man
                        fight
Why has that gun
        gone off?
Probably they are
        shooting
                something
What will be the issue
        of this?
What will they do
        in this matter?
Had we been early
        we should have
                arrived
                by this time
Had you told me
        I should have been
                glad

Choose, for instance, the hour of deep sleep. Then only in some spare secret places do nodes flash and trains of light-points traverse the embedded sleepers, indicating local activity still in progress, though ultimately scarcely audible from the mouth. Within one such enclave we follow a group of lights some thousands strong pursuing a recurrent manoeuvre as if of some incantational dance like those I loved from childhood.

It is a good thing
        that you have tied up
        my goat
It was a good thing
        they finished
                that work
        before the rain
                came
They first made holes
        and then cut
                the poles
        to the right
                length
        and then put them
                upright
                in the ground
It is a good thing
        that you are there
        to oversee them

I learned all the tunes – or, I should say, they clung to my memory – almost without any effort of my own, like the words and phrases of my native language, so that I could whistle or sing, or deliver them through sand with the utmost facility. Now, see them superintend the beating of the heart and the state of the arteries so that through sleep the circulation of the blood runs as it ought. The great knotted headpiece of the whole sleeping system lies for the most part dark, and quite especially so the roof-span where rope sits high like a petrified organism, a muscle devoid of activity. Move it, change its position and arrangement, touch it, and you can learn its secrets and the many of its meanings. Create forms with it. Divide space with it.

I will first read a verse
and then you repeat
my words
in order
that you may learn it
thoroughly
and that you may not
forget it
It is a good thing
that you have learned
how to read
and write

It was a good thing
that they found
for me
a carpenter

This abcess is burst
and a very good thing
too

Occasionally lighted points flash or move there, but soon subside. Such lighted points and moving trains of lights are mainly far in the outskirts; they wink slowly and travel slowly. At intervals even a gush of sparks wells up and sends a train down the cord, though failing to arouse it, so that people say a person has 'aged', as if before he had 'aged' he had not already aged, as if he were innocent of age before. Where, however, the stalk joins the headpiece, there goes forward in a limited field a remarkable display: rope is the condensation of the problem of thread, which is composed of many fibres whose number nobody tries to establish. There's no such thing as time, just a dense constellation of some thousands of nodal points bursting out every few seconds into a short phase of rhythmical flashing, yet we may speak of the biology of time: at first a few lights, then more, increasing in rate and number with a deliberate crescendo to a climax, declining then and dying away. After due pause the efflorescence is repeated. With each such rhythmic outburst goes a discharge of trains of travelling lights along the stalk and out of it altogether into several branches. What activity is this? The managing of breath the while we sleep.

I have just
        arrived
The food is just
        cooked
I have just
        been reading
The parrot which I have just
        bought
        is lost

Exploring structure, we take some quick thing, open it, review the component parts, their interactions. So, unavoidably, we stop time. Examining structure you miss the most interesting aspect of life: time. Not the minutiae of the clock, but time as modification of the body. Cell division, for example, is time, since cells don't 'un-divide'. There's no going back. When you build an animal, it sprouts. Growing like a plant it makes arm, forearm, hand. Cells which divide last are hand and those which divide first make up arm. So by counting divisions cells 'know' which part they must build, and time weaves form. Individuality arises through ageing, experience, the accumulation of time. We build ourselves through the world and each through other, and this proceeds to death as the brain alters with experience. Take someone who has never played the violin and teach. It takes a while, but if you look in the sensory cortex at the 'hands of the brain' they grow very fast. Scan, and you can see after just one month the 'hands of the brain' are already much larger as the music grows. That's individuation, experience. If I hadn't done violin my 'hand' would've stayed the same.

They have just
finished building
my house
The curtain has just
fallen down
He has only just
got up

They have just
sold out all the
copies
of that book
Just
put it down

After some time an impressive transformation suddenly accrues. In the great darkened head-end spring up constellations of twinkling stationary lights and countless trains set off on manifold courses. Encountering turn on turn, we rise at times uncomprehending to applaud, at other times fall prostrate to endure the agonizing pains we feel in the depths of our hearts. It is as though activity from one of those local places which continued restless in the darkened main-mass suddenly spread far and wide and invaded all. We see the great topmost sheet of the mass, where hardly a light had twinkled or moved, become a sparkling field of rhythmic flashing points with trains of travelling sparks hurrying hither and thither where at times, by the margin of the sea, there are ghost markets.

Did those goats get out
    last night?
As a matter of fact
    they did not
    because I tied up
        the door
    when I heard them
Never mind
    read
Tell them
    that they will have
        to finish
    the house today

As a matter of fact
    I did not learn
    to write

They come together in the middle of the night and scatter at cockcrow. Men who attend them usually chance upon rare things such as the word 'mutter', which produces an image of a dark brown sack with folds. That's what I saw when I first heard the word. It is another name for something else. The vowel sound is the base; the consonants make up the general background setting of the word. I see the bend in the word, but the t and r sounds are dominant. Another time, I heard the bell ringing. A small round object rolled right before my eyes, my fingers sensed something rough like a rope. Then I experienced a taste of salt water, and something white. Dissolution may be swift. When I was a child the image I had of a soul was that of animal lungs and livers, which I often saw on the kitchen table.

a wink
        of sleep
a glimpse
        of light
a cloud
        of fire
a blinding fit
        of anger
an access
        of rage
an ecstasy
        of joy
water crowfoot
gathered
        in a bright cloud
                about him
in the throes
        of death
he does not see
        a stim
I slept not
        a wink
moodily reflecting
perhaps he would take
        a notion
he is daft
he was beside himself
        when he heard
                the news
while in that state
        of frenzy
when the sky
        is clouded
tea is not a soporific
        drink

an irascible man

Then comes the waking, and it is as if the galaxy stepped out in dance. Swiftly the head-mass becomes an enchanted loom where millions of flashing shuttles weave a dissolving pattern. The fiber employed derives from plants and is like that of which ourselves are warped, for heart is surrounded by the coronary plexus, that most vital of threads. Handling fibre we handle centuries and distance, and a dry leaf has a network reminiscent of what has already occurred. Age is the accumulation of cells producing molecules that effect too far, and, causing tissue to disintegrate, it grounds the vaulting brood.

Give my boy
some medicine
to cure
his sickness
When that house
shall have fallen
down
we will build
another

He had tried
very hard
to read
but it was too much
for him
He had finished counting
when the storm
came
and threw down
the house
Why
does he talk
so much?

You grow old through surfeit of division; irresistible winds in your veins rock and bring down awkwardly. I, I think that's what deters us all is the loss of, of, of ability. You fall prone to error: a vertigo that strikes stillness cruelly. It's terrifying. Nobody wants to, to go through that, nobody wants to experience too much. When the biology of your body breaks down, the skin has to be cut so as to give access to the inside. Later it has to be sewn back like memory, when it may house all knowledge. Memory is our comfort and our attire. Fashioned with our hands it is the accomplishment of our dreams and lapses; always a meaningful pattern though never an abiding one; a shifting harmony of sub-patterns. Pretend I'm lost and try to find me.

He came
          whilst I was looking
                    for him
He had hung up
          all the curtains
          whilst I was out
Have you ever mixed
          medicine
                    before?
Have you ever seen
          my garden?
Did you take pity
          upon her?
Have you ever sewn
          a waistcoat
                    before?
We were cultivating when
          the rain
          came down
We were going
          to the big town
          and had nearly reached
                    the lake
          when we heard of
          the revolt
                    there

I was then a small child, crouching over a swampy pond, watching tadpoles. Enormous, those almost frogs swarmed at the bank. Through the thin membrane covering their distended bellies, the tangle of intestines was clearly visible. Heavy with the process of transformation, sluggish, they provoked hand. Dredged to the shore with a stick, carelessly disturbed, their swollen bellies burst. The contents leaked out in a confusion of knots. Soon they were beset by flies, insects, spiders, infusoria, microscopic fungi, leaves, air-bubbles, bits of metal, grains of sand, and little stones, all of which have been descried in the translucent prison-house. It has been asserted that no fewer than eight hundred species of insects have been found in amber, some recognised as similar to existing species, but mostly belonging to extinct genera.

They returned
from the fight
after they had buried
all the dead
and laid
all the wounded
who could not walk
on stretchers

They were coming back
when we met them

I sat there, my heart beating fast, shaken by what had happened, for are we not all prone to error, all strangers at home? As the language changes course through time, a placename gets stranded, parched, cut off from the stream of meaning, until another inundation reach, reinterpret, and reanimate. The sound may have to be bent for this to happen, and the first sense left for ever irrecoverable, or the stuff of books, though locally, as stuff of lives, it stays a name, a pointer (maybe misleading) to the place.

If you be not wise
then have
(bitter)
memories
May you not have
the memory
of the deer
It is my earliest
recollection
Quite unexpectedly

And how often might sound and sense perform this wayward dance? Corruption of the name, they call it; but corruption is fertility. I have seen a fragment in which I noticed a part of the little people to the number of the mystic seven, and so transparent were the walls of their ancient prison-house that the form, the colour, the attitude of the little creatures were distinctly visible, and so beautifully had they been preserved by Nature's unerring and skilful agency, that you could fancy that they had been incarcerated but the day before, not cast in durance in their crystal prison long years ago by the irresistible gravity of the sluggish resin down the stems of ancient pines which, it may be, were once that forest slumbering now beneath the Baltic wave. What does it signify when a picture falls from the wall?

The train is a great
          invention
It would take
          a long time
                    to make up
                    my mind
          to do it

Observe what follows on the destruction of soft life and the boundless mystery of the content of softness: shorn of that connective tissue which gave them meaning, assertions thinned to noise, promises proved empty, threats were ignored, warnings unheeded, and none of your questions could be answered. Though surface of your voice exhale presence, it was just the same as confronting a broken stem with sap flowing out, provoked by an inexplicable inner process, a force only apparently understood. But never mind all this. What drew my notice was those rooms filled with a great number of foreign fowls, preserved in their lively and beautiful colours, whose brilliant appearances, freedom in their plumage, and animated attitudes, seem as natural in this lifeless state, as if they still breathed.

He will probably carry
        that box
They are probably selling
        meat
        in the market
I think he has agreed
        to build
        a cook's house
        for me
Let me go
        and see
        if they will bring
        an axe to cut
        these trees
                with

It is the emotional colouring of events renders them memorable, and speech may orient emotion and event through story, where the narrator directs the affective response at will. Recall that translucent topaz-coloured rope coiling gravely down the prehistoric coniferous trunks where those adventurous and antique little people worked and played, arresting them, securing them before they could evade their bright entanglement, then fastening and embalming them in a crystal tomb. Think, then, how in receiving lore through incident and air, the listeners were engrossed. Witness this never fully explored mystery of the interior, soft and perishable.

That sick
old
man is
very ill
He will probably
die
tonight
I believe you are
selling
books
What
has he said?
Probably he has asked
for a book
We have probably
got out of
the road
He has probably
done
counting

On fine summer evenings, especially on Sundays, the young people collected at the cross-roads in the village for dancing, while the old brought reminiscence. Ned Goggin, then, our professional fiddler, gave us slow airs and fast, and went home in the end with his pockets well filled. Some of the greatest lovers of music that I can now recall were among the most hard-working and prosperous of the people, but a tree can only supply water, silently and without apparent movement, to its summit, because of the great tensile strength of water, whereby an enclosed column of it will not shatter into fragments except under enormous tension. Hence the ruin signalled in a low staccato through hushed forests during spells of drought: the sheer water columns click as they break inside the trees. The meeting-place survives, but it is desolate.

Leave off
        just there
My book
        is infinitely
        nicer
        than yours
The dog
        is completely
        lost
        perhaps it has hid
                itself
        in the long grass
He pushed
        me
        into the water

See the particular make memorable, and how certain spatial constructions, for example a building or the human body, have a coherence and logic to them through which one idea reaches unobstructed to another. I well remember that, in all the preparations of still life in these collections, the feathers were remarkably free, fine in colour, and equal in every respect to life itself. Impressed by the lively, active, striking, and emotionally charged images of this collection, I was determined to make a trial with a few birds upon this single thought, that many good old housewives preserve hams, beef, tongues, etc. for a long time with salt only. Consider, too, that at last the amber-weeping trees which ministered to that small commonwealth destroyed it, and yet preserved too its tiny citizens, as, gouged out of the ocean bed by profound tides, they surface in their transparent caskets, to be secured by the trawler's seine or by some seashore wanderer, after the mighty storm has wrenched yield from the wave.

His pleas
will be heard
later
Our work
will be greatly
increased

There are still some old people to the fore who, like myself, can recall the great snow and wind storm of the 15th February, 1838. It began in the morning and continued coming down in volumes without intermission all that day and night. About 11 o'clock that morning, Ned Goggin, on his way to his home up in the mountain gap, called at our home for shelter till the cold rustling on the road should cease. To avert evil, the village women had inscribed on their doors signs and letters with consecrated chalk and charcoal, and I longed to know the spells though they were inaccessible to me, as only their presence could mark off those cavities which were safe from those open to all sorts of forces. Sometimes the object can be a vessel.

I'd allow
        you
        to sow
                that field
                with oats
The people
        were slain
        all to a single
                three
I have a good back
        in the country
so I defy
        my enemies
Back of god-speed
There's no cloth
        left
        not the size
                of the black
                of my nail

Call to mind a space, perhaps schematic but usually architectural, which contains the various things to be remembered. Specific ideas there are nested within other more general notions, by virtue of being in niches within rooms. Certain advocates devote much energy to devising structures which in themselves have special meanings, so that the shapes of rooms and the ways in which they are connected form a three-dimensional semantic net, perhaps, but made memorable by being given concrete form as an imaginable physical building, a note from your beloved. Undistracted by such remote commotion, Ned sat by the kitchen fire till he was well thawed out, and then to our great delight he drew out his fiddle from its case, and began to play.

All these bones
          are to be picked
                    up
          by the boys
This house
          is to be pulled
                    down
This syrup
          is not to be drunk
          by the dog
This medicine
          is not to be drunk
          at once

I picked up on the beach many specimens of various hues, from pale lemon or straw-colour to a rich hyacinth-red all of which we fed the fire, and saw it burn with a bright flame, whereby often we discerned insects within. And all the while the snow fell thickly, drift on drift, while, infinitely cold, the unhinged king held sway over each slightest subject within memory. Still however much he attended to the literal shapes of knowledge, the settling drifts obscured structures left open to the elements, creating obvious gaps in the ordonnance, and though with information mapped to these finite, structured environments, omissions are glaring, yet even here, we are always in the intimate presence, its breath brushing the skin.

Why are you
        in such a blazing
        hurry?
A rude tambourine
        (from the bothered
        or indistinct sound)
I'll send you
        all the books
        and manuscripts
                box
                and dice
He is broken
        horse
        and foot
The hag
        of the ashes

Our information structures are now routinely too complex to be mapped deliberately onto great architectural spaces, and the landscape lies faulted with accidents, trysts and massacres. Small wonder, then, that placenames are semantically forked: denoting not only the specific place, they breed also connotation, a condensed or elliptic remark about that place, a description, a claim of ownership, an historical anecdote, even a joke or a curse on it. Thus, you and I can take different tours of the same space of ideas. Alone and together, we create and recreate landscapes: not just the earth but also the human, the land with its overplus of meanings. Take, for example, the word 'egg' I told you about before. It's so easy to lose sight of it; now I make it a larger image, and when I lean it up against the wall of a building, I see to it that the place is lit up by having a street lamp nearby. I don't put things in dark passageways anymore. Much better if there's some light around. It's easier to spot then.

I am not going
        to work now
I shall work
        in the morning

Tune followed tune, till at last Ned struck up The Tuning of the Colours, which delighted us, for the air is a beautiful minor one, and he played it well. I was then only 11 years old, and, of course, could not write music; but he played it over and over till the shapes I built grew soft and concealed everything that I now discover in imagination. Neither through the eye nor the hand that informs the brain can this be explained: the inside has the same importance as the outer shell, which is each time shaped responsive to the meat, while surface fashions depth: only together do they form a whole. When the wind blows and the flame goes out, at that time it rests on the wind. The interior invisible, which can only be guessed at matters as much as were it open for everyone, allowing actual penetration.

We will read
 every day
 in the afternoon
When shall we learn
 to write?
We shall soon
 learn
I once went
 to Europe
 but I do not now
 remember
 what I saw
 there

Contrast, then, true place, with all its affective wealth of memory and loss, with 'location' as fixed in terms of latitude and longitude or of a six-figure map reference or somesuch imposed, uniform schema. The lords of these nostalgic terraces, assisted by their lime-burners, masons and builders, used every possible device to haunt them with the user's memory, including washes of colour to distinguish one part from another, the use of elaborately distinct columns rather than a uniform design to prevent confusion, and even the glamour of numbers to entice the tremulous. Yet, in such a blizzard, often the subject went astray and was often lost, and if this teeming population strike you as dull, remember that the little folk generally sleep the winter through. Our violent and unceremonious entrance, and, to them, our equally unaccountable attack, together with the sudden shock of light, cause them to start up and look about them, thinking and hoping it all a dream, perchance; but no! all is reality; the attack is repeated, and both themselves and their winter quarters are removed by means of what to them would appear a lever of curious shape and monstrous size.

What do you want?
I am come
for some medicine
for my child
Where is he lying?
At my house

How old is he?
When was he taken ill?
On Sunday
Four days
ago.
What is the matter
with him?
He has headache
and is very
feverish
Has he much
pain?
Why did you not come
the day before
yesterday?
I did not know
that he was sick
It was last night
that I was told
of it

Some being crushed the while, dismay spreads throughout the colony; not a few run hither and thither in the echoing apparatus to ascertain the cause of the fatal intrusion. They gaze in wonder at the two grim giants working the implement of aggression, forgetful how to find the beast is precisely not to search for it. Terror-stricken, they seize their tender eggs, and endeavor to save them.

Where do you live?
Is it far away?
I had better come
        and see him
You must wait for me
        as I do not know
        the way
Here is the medicine
        for him
Give him one
        table-spoonful
                at a time
        three times
        a day
You can come again
        and see him
        the day after
        tomorrow
I will come again
        and see him
        the day after
        tomorrow

The efforts of the many are, however, unavailing; they are secured, imprisoned, and together with their young, their curious neat, and the varied chambers of their intricate domicile, placed in a receptacle with which we had provided ourselves. The salt and lime works may only reveal their meaning in the physical and historical context of place and age; it's just another name for something else. I have lately saved some scores of both land and sea fowls after this new method, all of which come as near real life as possible; therefore to gratify those who are pleased with this study and innocent employment, I shall now insert the whole apparatus necessary to be observed, and if these hints can draw their attention, my pleasure will be complete.

He is the sick person
for whom medicine
was fetched
on Wednesday?
He is well
He is gone to work.

How is your son
today?
He is better
Has he a good
appetite?
You may leave off
giving him
the medicine
I shall not come
to see him
any more

The colonists, numbered by hundreds, if not by thousands, with their countless little ones, their stock through the flickering of the fields whispering, and the corridors, the saloons, the dormitories, and the nurseries of their well-appointed, marvellously constructed messuage, were, on my return from my successful raid, deposited in a glass vessel, not twelve inches in diameter and in depth. Do not think it coincidental that memory should begin to fail just as taxonomies become a prominent tool for thought.

The house
        caught fire
        at midnight
We shall soon
        build
        another
Shall we build
        a temporary
        hut?

In a taxonomy, for example a zoological family tree, the structure arises out of the subject matter, rather than being arbitrary. With this in mind, I open the venter, from the lower part of the breastbone down to the anus, with a pair of fine-pointed scissors, and extract all the contents, such as the intestines, liver, stomach, etc. This cavity I immediately fill with the following mixture of salts and spice, and then bring the lips of the wound together by suture, delicately as it were the finest wedding dress, so as to prevent the stuffing from falling out. The gullet or diamond of the throat must then be filled, from the beak down to where the stomach lay, with the same mixture (but finer ground) which must be forced down a little at a time by the help of a quill or wire. The head I open by breaking through stars near the root of the tongue with the scissors, and after having turned them round three or four times to destroy the structure of the brain, I farce this cavity likewise with the mixture.

I am at work
    every moment
at times
    I am tired
        but that is nothing
    it is a very
        happy
        work

The assertion of Solomon, that the subjects of our contemplation are a little, a very little people, was amply vindicated in the unweathered calcite of innumerable fossils. The detached piece skewed along the mouth of a matching recess running in from the cliff's edge. Half a fossil coral showed in the lower left-hand face of the block, its counterpart in the right-hand wall of the recess. As evidently some wave had knocked that fragment from the rim, spun it on its axis and dropped it almost inverted back, can it surprise you that there are often flying heads among these torrents and grottoes?

I quite forgot it
I gather
        my thoughts
heed
        what I am about
He did not advert
        to what he was doing
        or saying
                (it was a slip)
They cherished
        the old spite
                against him
Reflect
        on the day
                of Judgment

Detached from its substrate long before, by successive ages of shocks and blows, fluctating heat and cold, and by trickling solvent waters, on the day before one's head is about to fly, a scar encircles the neck going right round the nape, like a red thread. Inevitably some future winter storm will mount the sixty or seventy feet of cliff and flip the splinter from its present awkward rest, where now the wife and children watch and are his mind, and someday yet another will shunt it in to join its accumulated predecessors on the storm beach. But when night comes, he seems to fall ill; his head suddenly sprouts wings, separates itself from the body and goes away. Then it searches for food such as crustaceans and worms in the mud of river banks. Straight before daybreak it flies back. Deeds leave their traces which give form to thirst, becoming tendencies, a drift. Just so: he wakes as from a dream, but now his belly is full.

He did that before
    he bathed
He did that after
    he had bathed
I wept
    when he died

These faces tell a story about something that is fluent in time and in material consistency; many times passing all at once in the same face; many existences side by side, together with experiences etched in the skin, and what you've lost, you can never be rid of. These faces unveil elements of the inner chaos hidden behind the living face just as is the makeup of the clown unique to each individual. Recall that the various expressive patterns were traditionally registered, and were recorded, each inscribed meticulously on an egg, but, alas, this precious laughing clutch hatched barren in the great blitz. Always the need is to search for and reveal secrets, such as that which, at the very instant of its surfacing and almost coming under the apprehension of the eye, is gone, either too late or too soon, a fleeting thing, already vanished. Also those inherent in structure; that being the phenomenon which all the organic world on our planet has in common, the mystery which can never be fully revealed. Never smile at a dog: they think you bare your teeth to snarl.

However foolish
    one may be
    if he were
    to continue
        reading
    ever so little
        (it may be)
    every day
    he will
        in the end
    improve his learning
    as the saying is
        a stone
        becomes
            hollowed
        through
        the crawling
            of ants

The wings and thighs I never touch, but leave them in their natural state; for the salts, etc. seldom fail, in a few days to penetrate into these parts, and preserve them equally with the body and neck. The bird thus filled with this antiseptic mixture must now be hung for about two days by the legs, that the salts may more effectually penetrate round the muscles and ligaments which connect the vertebrae of the neck. Do not, however, think me unaware that those who float their lives away aboard boats or greet old age leading horses, spend their days in travel and make travel their domicile. Many men of old died on the road. I too – from what year was it? – have been tempted by a solitary cloud drifting in the wind and, dissatisfied in my dreams of vagabondage, have wandered on the seacoast. The fowl must, nonetheless, be placed in a frame to dry, in the same attitude we usually see it when alive on the plain or on a tree; in this frame it must be suspended by two threads, the one passing from the anus to the lower part of the back, and the other through the eyes; the ends of these threads are to brace up the fowl to its natural attitude, and fastened to the beam of the frame above: lastly, the feet are to be fixed down with pins or small nails.

When speaking

what sort your voice is

let it be that sort

when you read

In that very autumn, I brushed away the old cobwebs from my ramshackle cottage on the river; and gradually as that year too came to a close and mists rose in the sky with the coming of spring, I grew of a mind to cross the boundary between states; a wanderlust engrossed both things and me; being directed by the gods of the road, no object I took in my hands stayed put. I could, of course, have thrown a rope across the ocean, but it's so exhausting travelling.

The firm
        has failed
What are
        the assets?
Show me
        a balance-sheet
My samples
        are delayed

With the exception of your neurons and your muscles, the cells of your first body are long gone. All else is new. Evidently, then, the question of what is an individual is a difficult one to settle, and yet a certain round boulder lying on the shore by the landing stage challenges the young men to lift it, and prompts boasts about their fathers or grandfathers who had done so before. The fear of physical failure, of eviction, emigration or the workhouse, must have clung in the night-hours like a cry of despair, satisfying the requirement that images be lively, active, striking, and charged with emotional affects to enter into the storehouse of memory. At the first bend I looked back and she was standing at the door. Years passed; I was in the capital, diligently recalling all my tunes for a noted antiquary, but The Tuning of the Colours had not yet come forward: translated from one place to another it grew old. Bearing its own story within itself, it contributed this to its surroundings, and in cities became an echo of the banished organic world.

Act of mourning
        lamenting
        wailing
        deploring
The form
        of metre
                used in
        deploration
Requiring to be lamented
        :dead

Mildness
smoothness
gentleness

Today, it allows one appraise architecture with all its artifice of hard decorative shell, while its own strength is that of every intertwined element, such as those in a tree, a human hand, or a bird's wing – all built of countless cooperating parts, and yet it might have been forgotten utterly and lost for good but for a history (not know which) shattering sleep. (Attend the flickering pad in that instant between stepping and lifting, where existence and time fall in.) In the middle of one winter night, the great snow with Ned Goggin and his music passed before me – trem neul, as the song-writers would say – "through my dream"; and as the waking body roused, with sub-patterns of this great harmony of activity stretching down into the unlit tracks of the stalk-piece of the scheme, I woke up actually whistling the tune. Strings of flashing and travelling sparks engaged the lengths of it. Greatly delighted, I started up – a light, a pencil, and a bit of paper, and there was the first bar securely captured: the bird was, as it were, caught and held by the tail, the gauger caught and thrashed, and the body was up, rising to meet its waking day.

Remove
        the stones
        with a crowbar
Blast out
        the rock

Bring the line
        and pegs
        to mark out
        the foundation
I shall come
        frequently
        and see
        how the work
                is progressing

As I have found two unrelated tribes residing in different parts of the same hillock, so I have found them peacefully located under the same stone near Stonehouse, and also in the neighbourhood of Minehead, the different species, however, keeping quite distinct establishments under the common roof. (This man, this leaping meat, carries his childhood within him like a sequestrum.) I dislodging the stones and disturbing the two colonies, the two species, pouring out of their respective chambers to ascertain the cause of the disturbance have not unfrequently met, and a desperate conflict has ensued, the unhappy consequence, possibly, of a misunderstanding having sprung up as to the occasion of their discomfort, and each attributing it to the unwarrantable interference of its next neighbor. Another trick, as one philosopher has urged, is to carve the bird at its joints.

Put aside
all stones
suitable
for the foundation
Let the doors
and windows
be well
fitted
The plastering
of the wall
must be done
neatly
White ants
will attack
the timber
tar it

And so, dissolving pattern after dissolving pattern will, the long day through, without remission melt into and succeed each other in this scheme by which for the moment we figure these things. In the thick drift, the spoor, the traces of the pack are sensible, but only by slow diligence abruptly can the pursuer ever arrive where the beast inhabits its own trace, see memory thicken and peel off like bark, watch the blazed world spin away. The forms of expression change. Only they can tell the truth about themselves. Pretend I am and find.

It is payable
at sight

Genealogies. The elementary tables. Dictionaries, assembled in blind frosts. Grammar and chronology. Libraries. Index: the Encyclopaedia, damascened with ice. So is the perfect body of knowledge dislimned. The rare thing exists because it does not stagnate but moves from one style to another. Especially, and with complexity incredible, in that object of our scrutiny, high at the roof.

Blood is no cure
          for thirst
The begetting of a son
          is the medicine
          for death
Take it!
          cures
          Give me!
Separation
          cures
          hatred

Head eats. Head looks. Head speaks. Listening to him it was as though a flame with fibres protruding from it advanced right towards me. I got so interested in his voice, I couldn't follow what he was saying.

There is a distant
        judgment
        leave off
                false dealing
        leave off
                whispering
        leave off
                jealousy
                and tale-bearing

Be afraid
        it is a day of meeting
        it is a day of shame
        whatever you are
                within
        shall be revealed
There is hiding
There is crouching
There is wrong-doing

In this situation all must remain for a month or more, until the bird is perfectly dry (which will be readily known by its stiffness). Like a flame, beyond any necessary substrate, even here is the spoor in the making of something more elusive, that burns faster than mind; urgent intent for which the beast incessantly yields up its only material, the system of stone traffic. Then it may be taken out of the frame, and placed on a chip pill-box: it will now require no other support but a pin through each foot, fastened into the box. But have you not heard this already?

On another day
            he is confused
            he is sorry
            he did not do it
Leave off repenting
            like a wildcat
                        it repents
                        with the fowl
                                    in its mouth
                        it puts it not down
Repentance
            like that of the wildcat
            is not enough
            for anyone
                        he shall
                                    indeed
                        have
                        nothing but evil

                                    stripes
                                    and chains
He shall be bound
            with his hands
            behind
He shall be dragged
            and turned
            over and over
The fire shall include
            everything
There shall be
            no getting away
                        from it

One who wished to absorb memory into logic particularly abjured the use of imagination, or any assistance provided by striking and stimulating images: the tooth, the gaze, the lulling claw. Now, though, ineluctably, the eyes must be supplied with proportionable glass beads, fixed in with strong gum water. Common salt one pound, alum powdered four ounces, pepper ground two ounces, happily commixed in airs: solitude and death.

He shall be dragged
and beaten
till the pain
is increased
in the squeezing
crushing
and great pain
He cries
He gasps for breath
in the pain
He is bowed
down
He is struck
frequently
as a skin
(that is beaten)
Again he is taken
and tied
to a painful stake
he screams
he bends
like a young tree
There is indeed for ever
no release at all
Much less will death
take him away
so that he should go
to rest

Then the entertainment ended with reprise of its first episode. The orchestra suddenly discovered a lively snatch of music, the corps de ballet swept as a body across the stage until they arrived before His Majesty, where they knelt at his feet in slow awe, then turned and flitted away as quickly as they had come. (There's no such thing as time; it's just another name for something else.) Only after day was done would they again quiet down, lapse half-way to extinction, and fall again asleep, for then at last, at least for the roof portion, motor acts cease; it is released from the waking day and marshals its factors for its motor acts no more. White noise drifts down. The orchestra falls silent, the performance done.

It is you
who will kill
the other thief
He is not
in the dark house
Put from you
the sweet food
What your friend eats
is better for you
Are the things
we do not see
better than the things
we see

Some Notes to the Poems

The Poems of Sweeney Peregrine: In the Irish text *Buile Suibhne* we may read how Suibhne (Sweeny), while engaged at the Battle of Magh Rath (637 a.d.), fled the fight and became a gealt. A description of this *avis rara* is to be found in the thirteenth century Norse *Speculum Regale*: "It happens that when two hosts meet and are arrayed in battle-array, and when the battle-cry is raised loudly on both sides, that cowardly men run wild and lose their wits from the dread and fear which seize them. And then they run into a wood away from other men, and live there like wild beasts . . . then feathers grow on their bodies as on birds. Their swiftness is said to be so great that other men cannot approach them, and greyhounds just as little as men. For these people run along the trees almost as swiftly as monkeys or squirrels."

The early Irish law tract, the *Book of Aicill*, which may be regarded as a product of the tenth century or earlier, remarks that: "Suibhne Geilt having become mad is not a reason why the battle [of Magh Rath] is a triumph but it is because of the stories and poems he left after him in Ireland." It would seem, then, that the tradition of Sweeny's madness and of his poems goes back perhaps to as early as the seventh or eighth century. The text, as it survives, seems somewhat the worse for *lacunae* and the pious interpolations of monks; the former have at least the virtue of reinforcing the sense of Sweeny's stress and distress. That text has been edited by J.G. O'Keeffe (1913 and 1931) and it is from his labour that this note and the accompanying working have borrowed their small gloss.

The relation in which the *Poems of Sweeny Peregrine* stand to the original Irish of *Buile Suibhne* may perhaps best be described by that phrase which Clarence Mangan used of his own inventive translations: they are "the antithesis of plagiarism."

Fast Rivers: This echoes three of the Coplas of Jorge Manrique (c.1440-1479).

The Turlough: The turloughs or winter lakes of western Ireland occur in areas of karstic limestone. Rain falling on this land drains away through swallow-holes or sinks, but precipitation anywhere within the watershed may cause the water-table to rise again above the valley floor, whereupon streams issue through the crevices by which they had previously drained away.

The rhyme London Bridge is Falling Down is taken to refer to the ancient practice of burying alive a watchman beneath a newly-built bridge to prevent the stones being washed away.

Observation of the red shift in the spectra of distant stars revealed that the universe is expanding. If the total material in the universe exceeds a critical mass, gravity will eventually halt its expansion and the universe will implode for another big bang. Should the universe ever start to contract, this would be evident in a blue shift.

Verses with a Refrain: The specific Christ referred to bestrides the Anastasis on the paracclesion wall at Kariye Camii, Istanbul.

Lines in Fall: These take on the voice of the first two Autumn Meditations by Meng Jiao (751-814).

Orrery Hill is situated in Cork city where it rises just above Sunday's Well. It is presumably named after one of the Boyle family who were earls of Orrery. It was under the patronage of Charles Boyle, the fourth earl, that the device known as an orrery was invented. This is a mechanical model of the solar system used to demonstrate the motions of the planets around the sun.

Tenters are tenter-hooks, used for stretching cloth after manufacture. The first corporation housing estate built in Dublin is still known familiarly as 'the Tenters' because it is sited on the Tenters' Fields, which were used by the Huguenot textile-makers of Weavers' Square.

Cold Course: "As soon as the First Emperor became king of Qin, excavations and building had been started at Mount Li . . . They dug through three subterranean streams and poured molten copper for the outer coffin, and the tomb was filled with models of palaces, pavilions and offices, as well as fine vessels, precious stones and rarities. Artisans were ordered to fix up crossbows so that any thief breaking in would be shot. All the country's streams, the Yellow River and the Yangtse were reproduced in quicksilver and by some mechanical means made to flow into a miniature ocean. The heavenly constellations were shown above and the regions of the earth below." (Sima Qian on the First Emperor of China)

Elixir poisoning was a not uncommon way of death amongst classical Chinese emperors and their courts. These elixirs were taken in the pursuit of physical immortality. Vermilion (or cinnabar), a compound of mercury, was amongst the most frequently used, and it induced ulceration, vomiting of blood, and agonising pain, and mercury excreted in the sweat or urine could often be retrieved from the sheets or mattress of the victim. Gold was also ingested for this purpose.

Coumeenole: This is the name of a strand at the western end of the Dingle peninsula, opening out onto the Atlantic from under Slea Head.

Tocharian Music: The Tocharians were an ancient people who spoke an Indo-European language and whose cities in central Asia lay on the Buddhist pilgrim route between China and India. Their rebellion against Chinese rule and the subsequent reprisal which devastated their culture occurred in the mid-seventh century. Wandering throughout Asia, their famous dancers and musicians continued after the ruin of these kingdoms to influence the greatest period of Chinese poetry and music during the Tang dynasty. Written scores of their own music have come down to us, but lacking the necessary indications of tempi.

Cry Help: This is worked from the Irish of Aogán O'Rathaille (c.1675-1729) at the request of Brian Coffey.

Chimaera: Both this poem and The Turlough each deploy certain features of the Japanese renga form, which uses systematic ambiguity to chain together a series of brief stanzas every one of which hinges both forward and backward. This form was often used in Japan for joint composition by several poets. Chimaera is such a composite, for three voices, plaiting the disparate ghosts of Richard Lovelace (1618-57), Aloysius Bertrand (1807-41), and the original author and later interpolators of the Lie-zi. There is interference on all channels.

Tohu-bohu: Thunder Perfect Mind is one of the volumes comprising the Gnostic library found under the sands at Nag Hammadi.

The final section incorporates a number of technical terms used in computer networking.

A niptic cat would share the watchful qualities exemplified by the Niptic Fathers of the Philokalia, a collection of texts written during the fourth to fifteenth centuries by spiritual masters of the Orthodox Christian tradition.

'93/4: Algol is a binary star in the constellation Perseus in which it was often taken to represent the head of Medusa. The name derives from the Arabic Al Ghul, the demon or mischief-maker, as it was understood to be the most baleful star in the heavens. ALGOL was the first procedural computer language.

Art Ó Laoghaire, whose murder on May 4th., 1773, is mourned in the fine lament attributed to his widow, lies buried in Kilcrea Abbey, some fifteen miles west of Cork.

Dogen Kigen (1200-53), Japanese poet, philosopher and founder of Soto Zen.

Tao Qian (c.365-427), Chinese poet and gardener.

The immense monument of Borobodur, in Java, contains the images of many buddhas. Those near the base are clearly visible in the open while those at the penultimate level as one ascends the world-mountain are almost hidden in great bell-shaped lattices of stone, or stupas. The single stupa which stands at the highest point is completely closed, and inside it was found by its restorers an image of the buddha, whose rudimentary unfinished form is generally taken to indicate the only partial presence in our realm of a supreme buddha.

The great Hindu god, Indra, carried a net as part of his divine kit. Every intersection of this net was marked by a jewel, each of which simultaneously reflected all the others, so that the entirety was fully there at each point, though from a different perspective. The image of the Jewel Net of Indra was often used in Buddhism to indicate the essential connectedness of things, and their consequent emptiness when taken in isolation.

Golden Master: In software development, Golden Master is the ultimate stage of the code, when all testing is finished, all changes are incorporated, and all known bugs have been eliminated. At this point, version numbers are set to the final release numbers, and the disks are duplicated, archived, and sent to manufacturing.

In Greek mythology, King Midas could only rid himself from the divine gift of having everything he touched turn to gold by bathing in the river Pactolus, whose sands have ever since been thick with gold dust.

Hearsay: The burial vaults and Norman tower are part of St. Michan's church. The friary referred to is St. Mary of the Angels. Both are located in Church St., Dublin.

Syzygy: In the mediaeval musical form known as cancrizans, one or more parts proceed normally, while the imitating voice or voices give out the melody backwards. The name derives from *cancer,* the Latin term for a river-crab or sea-crab, though, as one authority observes, crabs tend to move sideways rather than backwards. This palindromic form came into use in the fourteenth century, and surfaced again in the serial music of our own time.

David Munrow notes, of Guillaume de Machaut's *Ma fin est dans ma commencement*, that "the words of the popular mediaeval aphorism provide less of a text than instructions for performance" and, remarking that in such a canon "the words inevitably obscure the overall symmetry", he elected to go for a purely instrumental performance. In addition to the antecedent voice and the reversed consequent, Machaut had added a third voice which is itself compactly palindromic, moving from its opening to a point, exactly midway in the piece, from which it meticulously undoes itself, note by note, until it rearrives at its commencement.

In the present instance, the drift having been established, the identical voices are intermeshed to weave the palindromic net. This is roughly analogous to Machaut's canon, with the first four voices combining to produce the first line of each composite verse, the second four making the middle lines, and the final four contributing the last line of each verse. Here too, words obscure the symmetry, which was implemented using an industry-standard computer spreadsheet.

You already know a diamond is forever, and that gold is a noble and perfect metal. I can't now recall where to find the clearest account of how ideas of order, of exact cyclical repetition, were first derived from the periodicity of the stars.

According to a citation in the Opies' Dictionary of Superstitions, "on the East coast [of Scotland] the salmon is the red fish, the liberty fish, the foul fish, or simply the fish". Sometimes, 'salmon' being a taboo word, it was called 'The Beast'. The weather-cock on the top of St. Anne's Church in Shandon, Cork, is a giant salmon, indicating the importance of the fishing industry of the River Lee to the citizenry of two cenuries ago. The tower on which it sits summarises the neighbouring geology in its two faces of silver limestone, two of red sandstone. The turret-clock within is known locally as 'the four-faced liar' as each of its faces renders its own version of the time. In his paper on The Fish of Life and the Salmon of Life, the Swedish folklorist Bo Almqvist documents "the belief that the soul or principle of life manifests itself in the shape of a fish".

The first Emperor of China standardized measures in the subjugated lands, and his successors enclosed exotic game within 'intelligence parks' for hunting and amazement. Sir William Petty in his seventeenth-century Survey imposed a new taxonomic order on the territories of Ireland, completing their reduction. In the final chapter of her Purity and Danger, Mary Douglas describes how "the attitude to rejected bits and pieces goes through two stages. First they are recognizably out of place, a threat to good order, and so are regarded as objectionable and vigorously brushed away . . . This is the stage at which they are dangerous; their half-identity still clings to them and the clarity of the scene in which they obtrude is impaired by their presence. But a long process of pulverising, dissolving and rotting awaits any physical things that have been recognized as dirt. In the end, all identity is gone . . . So long as identity is absent, rubbish is not dangerous. It does not even create ambiguous perceptions . . . ."

The line "and then there is this sound the red noise of bones" is from the poem Agua Sexual in the second volume of Neruda's Residencia en la Tierra. Sean Ó Boyle records, when discussing The Irish Song Tradition, the curse of an old woman, having finished a song on the wreck of a fishing-boat on its way to the off-shore grounds: "the thieving sea, the thieving sea. They say it will go into three quart jugs on the day of Judgement". The fear that we may suffer a severe exposure was expressed in the financial pages of some paper I've long forgotten.

Hopeful Monsters: A 'Hopeful Monster theory' is defined by Terence Deacon in his book The Symbolic Species as "the evolutionary theorist's counterpart to divine intervention, in which a freak mutation just happens to produce a radically different and serendipitously better-equipped organism."

Approach of Bodies Falling in Time of Plague: Newton's most productive period, during which he arrived at many of his major discoveries concerning gravity and the composite nature of natural light, coincided with a severe outbreak of the plague. Newton in his later years was appointed Master of the Royal Mint.

Proceeds of a Black Swap: This term is defined in P.W.Joyce's English as we Speak it in Ireland: "when two fellows have two wretched articles – such as two old penknives – each thinking his own to be the worst in the universe, they sometimes agree for the pure humour of the thing to make a *black swop*, i.e. to swop without first looking at the articles. When they are looked at after the swop, there is always great fun."

Data Shadows: The 'data shadow' cast by an individual in a series of electronic transactions (via ATM, credit card or internet usage, for example) can be assembled into a pattern which will allow a profile of that person to be developed, including personal habits, and buying power and preferences. Information collected in one context is routinely reused in entirely unanticipated and even hostile ways without the knowledge or consent of the individual involved.

The structure, and much of the imagery, is drawn from the shamanic Summons of the Soul in the ancient Chinese collection, The Songs of the South.

behaviour self!: This was written for inclusion in A Book for Tom Raworth, to celebrate his sixtieth birthday. This piece and the three immediately preceding are constructed lattice-wise, their lines to be read in two distinct orders. Both orders are printed here.

Watch: Worked from an Hungarian folk-song.

Joinery: The ten non-indented lines constitute, in order, the whole of the second poem in Michael Smith's sequence Dedications.

Let Happen: The non-indented lines are extracted from Randolph Healy's poem The Rodin Sculpture Garden, Stanford. (Included in Ludo, no. 6 formSheet by Form Books.)

DARK SENSES PARALLEL STREETS: In the left column is Tom Raworth's poem DARK SENSES (included in his collection Clean and Well Lit). In the right column is my own PARALLEL STREETS, written so as to be read either as a separate text, or, alternatively, to be read across, its lines a continuation of Tom's, each of the sixty-four composite lines consisting of exactly eight words.

This and the two preceding poems are written *with* the dedicatees, only in the sense that they have generously permitted me to incorporate their lines among my own.

Trem Neul: This apparatus echoes and distorts many voices other than my own, and although it would be pointless to give a complete list, I would like to identify Magdalena Abakanowicz, Judith Campisi, Patrick Weston Joyce, A. R. Luria and 'S', M. MacDonald, Christy Moore, Alain Prochiantz, Tim Robinson and Sir Charles Sherrington as among the more recently sounding, contributing both shell and meat.

The Illustrations

The Poems of Sweeny, Peregrine

Map of the world, made in +787 by the Spanish monk, Beatus.

Pentahedron

An ancient graph, showing (according to Dr. L.Weiger, S.J., in his study of Chinese Characters) "presentation of a new-born babe, the fontanelle of whose skull is not yet closed, in the temple, with a libation." The graph dates from the period when Chinese script was itself in an early stage of development.

stone floods

A section of the Chinese First Emperor's terracotta army, in process of excavation.

Syzygy

Segment of the interior wall of the dove-cot or columbarium, immediately ESE of the church of Ballybeg Priory, Buttevant, County Cork.

Hopeful Monsters

Three exhibits from the eighteenth-century collection of Bernhard Siegfried Albinus, in the Boerhaave Museum at Leyden. "From left to right: a human embryo with surrounding membranes; a child's arm complete with a cambric sleeve trimmed with lace, the fingers holding the choroid membrane of the eye; and an ear."

Shorter poems

Facsimile specimen of the Senchus Mór, from P.W.Joyce's Social History of Ancient Ireland. The caption proceeds: "The four lines of large text are a part of the Senchus Mór proper; and they are to be read in the order, second, first, third, fourth. The commentary (i.e. the small text) consists of seventeen lines; and, supposing them to be numbered from top to bottom, they are to be read in this way:– Begin at line 8 (which comments on the line of larger text right under it); then 7, 6, 5; part of 4 and part of 3 (both as far as the curve); the rest of 4, the rest of 3; then 2, 1. Resume at 9 and go on in like manner – sometimes upwards, sometimes downwards – to the end; the reader being guided all through by the context" and concludes by noting that "no glosses occur on this Facsimile."

Trem Neul

Photographic negative, taken by Nora Joyce, showing a co-operative *meitheal* saving hay in Coolaghy, County Galway, c. 1950.